MUSIC FOR ELEMENTARY SCHOOL CH
MT 3 HEN93

P9-EAI-504

Date Due

FE 9 '88	OC 27 00	JE 1 0 09	
MR 7 '89	NO 17 00		
MY 4 '00	NO 29 00		
AP 17 '01	JE 19 01		
AP 19 '99	MY 17 '02		
MY 7 '98	AP 6 '05		
AP 14 '99	AP 27 '05		
MY 12 '99	FE 8 '07		
FE 2 '00	FE 1 1 09		
OC 2 '99	JE 4 '07		

MT
3
U5N93

Riverside City College Library
Riverside, California

1. All members of the community are entitled to use the library.
2. Reference books are to be used only in the library.
3. Reserved books and circulating books may be borrowed in accordance with library rules.
4. The date due will be stamped in each book loaned.
5. Injury to books beyond reasonable wear and all losses shall be paid for by the borrower.
6. No books may be taken from the library without being charged.

Music for
Elementary School Children

THE LIBRARY OF EDUCATION

A Project of The Center for Applied Research in Education, Inc.

G. R. Gottschalk, Director

Advisory Board:

Ralph W. Tyler, Chairman
James E. Allen, Jr.
C. Ray Carpenter
Harold C. Case
Theodore A. Distler
Henry H. Hill
Monsignor Frederick G. Hochwalt
Paul A. Miller
Harold G. Shane
Harold Spears

Editorial Board:

Walter A. Anderson, Chairman
John S. Brubacher
Eric F. Gardner
Daniel E. Griffiths
John Dale Russell

Categories of Coverage

I	II	III
Curriculum and Teaching	Administration, Organization, and Finance	Psychology for Educators

IV	V	VI
History, Philosophy, and Social Foundations	Professional Skills	Educational Institutions

Music for

Elementary School Children

ROBERT E. NYE

Professor of Music Education
University of Oregon

Riverside City College Library
Riverside, California

The Center for Applied Research in Education, Inc.
New York

© 1963 BY THE CENTER FOR APPLIED
RESEARCH IN EDUCATION, INC.
NEW YORK

ALL RIGHT RESERVED. NO PART OF THIS BOOK
MAY BE REPRODUCED IN ANY FORM, BY MIMEO-
GRAPH OR ANY OTHER MEANS, WITHOUT PER-
MISSION IN WRITING FROM THE PUBLISHERS.

Second printing. . . . . . . August, 1964

LIBRARY OF CONGRESS
CATALOG CARD NO.: 63-9762

PRINTED IN THE UNITED STATES OF AMERICA

Foreword

Dr. Robert E. Nye is well qualified to discuss the subject of music in the elementary school. His experience as a music educator has been equally divided between classrooms in the public schools of Illinois and Wisconsin, and in teacher training institutions in Alabama and Oregon. Dr. Nye has been particularly sensitive to the problems faced by elementary classroom teachers who are responsible for teaching their own music.

Though Dr. Nye has made a sincere and intelligent effort to improve the music training of the classroom teacher, he has also recognized her limitations as a music teacher. He has been a vigorous spokesman for the position that music training will best realize its full potential in the lives of children when it involves the services of a specialist teacher. In this monograph he reminds us that it does not matter who teaches music, but it does matter that the child receives the instruction in music to which he is entitled.

The author has stressed in this monograph the notion which is gaining increased favor among music educators that music should be justified in the schools primarily because what it can do for children, no other subject can do as well.

Another of the author's concepts with far reaching implications is his emphasis on the need for continuity in learning—continuity from activity to activity, from day to day, and from grade to grade. In application, this is one of the most damaging arguments against the self-contained classroom, for, even under very good conditions, the music teaching abilities of classroom teachers are so widely varied, that continuity is seldom achieved.

Dr. Nye's treatise will prove stimulating to all persons interested in improving the teaching of music in the elementary school. It will be read profitably by elementary classroom teachers, administrators, and by music teachers themselves, and will have provocative value in stimulating thoughtful discussion. It not only deals with practical problems in music education today, but, because of frequent reference to historical foundations of music in the schools, it gives the reader a valuable perspective.

KARL D. ERNST
Head, Division of Creative Arts
Alameda State College

Contents

Music for
Elementary School Children

CHAPTER I

Music in General Education

Music is considered an integral part of American education. Even before it became a recognized part of the curriculum, singing was often practiced in schools. In 1836 the Boston School Board granted the request of petitioners to include music as part of the educational program and stated that: "Through vocal music you set in motion a mighty power which silently, but surely, in the end, will humanize, refine, and elevate a whole community." [1] Lowell Mason, often termed "the father of music education in the United States," was the first officially employed school music teacher. He stated his teaching objectives for the new position as, "improving the affections, and enobling, purifying and elevating the whole man." [2]

Edward Birge, speaking of the inclusion of music in the official curriculum, comments:

> The fact that it could occur at a time when the value of a school subject in practical daily affairs was the criterion by which it was judged is evidence that music had become so strongly interwoven in community life that its utility would be taken for granted. [3]

Music was undertaken not as a talent-finder or as a cultural subject for the few, but as a subject with which, as part of the common cultural heritage, the entire citizenry was to become familiar. In 1910 Osbourne McConathy, distinguished music educator and author, said that every child ought to be educated in music according to his natural abilities, that the music he studies in school should relate to the use of music by the community—in the home, church, and in community music organizations, and that he should be educated at public expense. [4]

In 1948, Dr. Alexander Stoddard, then Superintendent of Schools

---

[1] Edward B. Birge, *History of Public School Music in the United States* (Philadelphia: Oliver Ditson Company, 1939), pp. 40-49.

[2] Gilbert Chase, *America's Music* (New York: McGraw-Hill Book Company, Inc., 1955), pp. 158-59.

[3] Birge, *op. cit.*, p. 35.

[4] Birge, *op. cit.*, p. 251.

1

in Philadelphia, described the expansion of music in the American Schools as follows:

> There was a time when music in the schools was regarded as a luxury, to be maintained if there were sufficient funds. Or it was regarded as something extra and not exactly as an integral part of the curriculum itself. Neither of these attitudes prevails any longer in most of our school systems and communities. We now generally regard music education as an essential part of our total education program both from the standpoint of its financial support and its contributions to the growth of our people, young and old. Music is no longer a frill. It is now one of the fundamentals in the program of the schools. Music has come to be a part of what is regarded as general education or the common learnings. It is closely related to history and other social studies. It is an integral part of our social mores and must be studied as such. It is one of the most fundamental means through which peoples have always expressed themselves and therefore helps to explain the political development of nations. Music is mathematical and scientific in its background although its greatest use is as one of the greatest of all arts developed by the human race. Thus it is that any consideration of what is called general education in our schools gives large place to music not as a side show but as an integral part of the total scheme.[5]

Music has not always been taught by methods which would warrant the public support indicated by the above statements. In the depression years of the 1930's, it was regarded as sufficiently peripheral in importance to be dropped from the list of subjects taught in many schools. Today many educators are pressured to introduce material values into education, to the detriment of human and spiritual values. Sterling M. McMurrin,[6] U.S. Commissioner of Education, indicated that in his opinion all schools should offer students opportunities in music and art. He stated that it was unfortunate that the arts are sometimes regarded as appendages to education rather than as a part of education itself, and added that the arts and the humanities are as important as the sciences in the education of people. When Commissioner McMurrin appointed Harold Dean Cator as consultant in education in the arts, he said that the arts should be

---

[5] Alexander J. Stoddard, excerpt from brief of an unpublished address delivered at the Music Educators National Conference, Philadelphia, 1948.

[6] Sterling M. McMurrin, "The Real Weakness in American Schools," *U.S. News & World Report* (August 28, 1961), 58-59.

given a prominent place in the educational process at all levels of instruction.[7]

The Commissioner's remarks reflect concern about the current status of music in general education. At present, music education seems to be in no danger of being removed from the curriculum. Serious questions, however, are being raised regarding its present status and its future. According to research, elementary school music has not kept pace with the degree of development demonstrated in most other subject areas. Although the principles constituting a good music program for children have been clearly defined, they have seldom been implemented. Therefore, it is evident that the role of music in the education of today's children is in need of careful analysis.

Purposes of music instruction. In 1956 Karl Gehrkens claimed that most school administrators and even some music teachers did not know why music should be taught to all children nor did they know what part music should play in general education.[8] Many music educators have given the impression that they were so occupied with teaching that they gave little thought to why music deserved a place in the curriculum. Ignoring to a large extent the philosophical thinkers in the field, they seemed content that music was firmly established in American education. They felt that this was so because music was acceptable in light of certain goals of general education such as good citizenship, health, vocational ability, recreational and spiritual values, self-discipline, and personality development—goals which music shares with other subjects. In recent years, however, a conviction has developed that unless music can be taught in ways which reveal its *unique* values, its current status might be in jeopardy. Music educators no longer limit justification of music education to the fact that it can do for children what many other subject areas may also do for them; they now seek primary justification by attempting to show that music can help children reach goals which no other subject can achieve, or which no other subject can achieve as well, or as efficiently.

It has been stated that man possesses many qualities to be developed through education—the major ones being social and cultural,

---

[7] "McMurrin Encourages the Arts," *Phi Delta Kappan* (January, 1962), 179.
[8] Karl W. Gehrkens, "Five Decades of Music Education," *Education* (March, 1956), 405.

physical and emotional, intellectual and aesthetic. To the extent that any man fails to develop his potential in any of these, he remains proportionately uneducated. Thus, no man is considered educated who is ignorant of the arts. In the opinion of this author, it is in the areas of aesthetics and cultural education that music education finds primary justification for inclusion in general education.

Aesthetics and music. The primary purpose of music in general education is to develop the capacities of children to respond to aural beauty with pleasure and with understanding. The educated man incorporates aesthetic principles into his daily living, and these contribute a quality factor which is necessary to healthy human behavior and which adds to human happiness. Appropriate musical experiences in the education of children should provide the means for satisfying the basic need to symbolize experience through an art medium. Creativity and good taste are two important elements in aesthetic education. Proper education in music will develop the ability to enjoy music with perception and discrimination.[9]

Music is a uniquely superior means by which to achieve the purposes of aesthetic education: first, because no other subject teaches aural recognition of beauty in the same way, and, second, because it lends itself better than any other art to the types of organized group participation that are characteristic of our educational system.

Cultural-social education and music. Another primary purpose of music education is to transmit the cultural heritage. Music literature is a significant part of this heritage. Although other areas of the curriculum are also engaged in achieving this general purpose, music can accomplish it in unique ways.

Since before the dawn of history, music has been the constant companion and confidant of man. Man has conceptualized his every experience by means of music. The study of folk music shows it to be a means of preserving the things men cherish, and reveals it as a key to understanding the lives, experiences, and values of people. Music is inseparable from the study of our own cultural heritage, or that of other societies and other times. It is a superior vehicle in teaching the humanities because the aural approach of music is an emotional approach which motivates learning. Music is a liberal

---

[9] Charles Leonhard and Robert W. House, *Foundations and Principles of Music Education* (New York: McGraw-Hill Book Company, Inc., 1959), p. 99.

art, and when taught as such is not dealt with in isolation, but as a part of the life and history of humanity. Therefore, no genuine program of general education can omit music.

Music is an art of social significance. It is also of decided importance in its effect upon the social outlook of children. Man is a social being who finds himself through his relations with others. Through group activities in music, the child may satisfy his need for acceptance, for belonging, and for success. In this way, music serves personality development. When the child finds pride and success through his cooperation with a group in musical activities, he is building social consciousness. Through music experiences he may become sensitive to the feelings of others, and understanding of the individual differences in ability which are normal in humanity. Another aspect of the social values of music is found in the area of recreation, for with the increase of leisure in American society, the values of music in recreation are increasingly significant.

Thus an important secondary purpose of music is its effect on social and personality development, and its contribution to a worthy use of leisure time by American adult society.

Health education and music.   Another secondary purpose of music education is found in its contribution to physical well-being. While this alone would not justify music's inclusion in the curriculum, it is but one of the many examples of music's versatility and its capacity to assist in or relate to other areas. Release from physical tension at frequent intervals is a necessity for growing boys and girls. Through action songs, singing games, dances, rhythmic dramatizations, and other bodily responses to music, this need can be satisfied whenever it appears in the school day. Rhythm is an essential element of music: children need to learn to control their bodies with ease, confidence, and grace, and music can serve this purpose. The study of wind instruments may increase lung capacity and breath control.

Music is a superior means through which the child expresses his emotional reactions to his world; it can provide exhilarating outlets for natural and spontaneous self-expression, religious feelings, and successful creative activities. The aesthetic impact of beautiful tone can evoke deep emotional response. Children need to develop the capacity to express their personal emotional responses under the type of skilled guidance which leads toward wholesome development. Music can thus contribute to both physical and mental health.

Intellectual education and music.   Purposes in this area are centered around (1) knowledge, and (2) understanding and appreciation. Knowledge of music should come primarily from the study of the music itself—what it communicates and by what musical means this communication takes place, such as melody, harmony, rhythm, form, instrumentation, and style. This knowledge is essential in serving intellectual purposes such as the broad goals of musical understanding and appreciation. Thus, certain extrinsic knowledge, such as facts about composers, is not as important as the knowledge which is gained from the explorative study of the music itself.

Understanding is measured by the ability to use musical knowledge and skill to solve problems which arise in musical experience. Such problems may arise from experiences in listening, performance, note-reading, composition, or improvisation. Because music is such a vast field of intellectual endeavor (it even relates to science through acoustics and to mathematics through both acoustics and music theory), it can be said to possess as much intellectual content as any other area of education. Therefore it can serve intellectual goals very well. In practice, music teaching should maintain a balance between emotional foundations on one hand and intellectual knowledge and understanding on the other. The proper balance results from the teacher's understanding of the characteristics of the age group of the children being taught, and their musical background.

Technical purposes of music education.   Two primary purposes of music education and some of the numerous secondary purposes have been discussed. However, in order to progress toward these indicated goals, musical skills and technical understandings must be developed. Since all of the areas discussed are interrelated, technical aspects of music can be taught logically in functional relation to them. It should be emphasized that *music skills are essential in order to realize the many purposes of music instruction.* For example, bad singing tone, out-of-tune singing, and lack of rhythmic consistency or of listening skills can very effectively prevent the realization of teaching goals in both aesthetics and in understanding our cultural heritage through music. Lack of a reasonable understanding of notation is a deterrent to the increasing of knowledge of music literature. Lack of skill in analyzing the musical means employed by a composer or arranger to communicate through sound blocks the fulfillment of teaching purposes related to listening activities. The teaching of music skills, therefore, has an essential place in any legitimate instructional program.

It should be kept in mind that when a child comes to school he brings his entire being—his aesthetic, social, cultural, physical, emotional, and intellectual self. Each of these aspects of his makeup is either enhanced or retarded by the others. Herein lies the necessity for proper balance in the general education of children, a balance which includes music as an essential area of study. Also, since the area of music contains so many facets, a balance of experiences is necessary within music itself. As in all areas of the curriculum, teacher competency in music is necessary if musical learnings are to take place in the classroom. Therefore, the most essential factor in attaining the goals which can be reached through instruction in music is the teacher, who must be educationally and musically competent.

CHAPTER II

The Developing Music Curriculum

In the nineteenth century, music instruction was devoted to objectives concerned with singing. Teachers endeavored to accomplish two things: to teach children a large repertoire of songs by rote, and to teach them to read notation so that they might expand their acquaintance of music literature as independent learners. Teachers and laymen alike wished to develop in children sufficient note-reading skill so as to permit enjoyment of congregational singing in the churches, and encourage eventual participation in church choirs and community choruses.

In the early part of the twentieth century, a number of developments took place concurrently. One was the mass production and marketing of recordings. The phonograph, which had been invented by Thomas A. Edison in 1877, became popular. Music teachers seized upon this as an effective way in which to introduce children to music that they otherwise might not hear. Early experimenting with this new educational aid produced a type of activity which depended largely upon children's memorization of melodies which led in turn to the identification of titles and composers of selections heard. "Music memory" contests were briefly popular. Because this factual approach to listening was based upon extrinsic values such as titles and names and not upon the values of the music itself, it failed to produce the appreciation for music which had been expected. In this failure of methodology, teachers of music, as well as teachers of other subjects who used the same factual approach in their respective fields, found that effective teaching involved more than demanding the memorization of facts and that more understanding of the learning process was necessary. The record player, however, became an indispensable part of school equipment and listening to recordings was established as an addition to the music curriculum. It is possible that certain newly introduced teaching machines of today which rely exclusively upon similar memorization may meet with similar difficulties. Fortunately, teachers can learn from experience and improve their methods; machines may not be as flexible!

There have always been outstanding teachers—many of them unknown—who have been far ahead of their own time. One of them is Mrs. Satis Coleman, who taught music at Lincoln School, Teachers College, Columbia University, in the 1920's. She believed that children should live the art of music from its primitive beginnings—an application of the theory that children should, in their education, somehow recapitulate creatively the history of the race. Under her guidance, the children made their own primitive instruments which they struck or plucked. Her aim was a curriculum based upon the historical evolution of music, in which the making and playing of instruments merged with dancing, singing, and the composition of poetry.[1] Original music was composed by the children as a natural outgrowth of the learning environment. Mrs. Coleman stressed the fact that there was a musical instrument to match the capacity of every child, and that experience with simple instruments should precede experience on the piano and other complex instruments. Acceptance of her ideas is still growing, and eventual complete acceptance seems assured.

The music curriculum today.   *Singing* is regarded as the most basic of the different activities comprising the present-day music curriculum. It is asserted that the human voice is a musical instrument everyone carries with him at all times; thus it is a naturally superior means of making music. To sing a song well requires much concentrated thought on the part of teacher and children. Studying the words of a song helps in deciding the type of tone quality that is necessary to convey properly the thought to be expressed. It is quite possible that each line or phrase of a four-stave song can require different gradations of tone quality to express adequately the meaning of those phrases. Since it is imperative that the thought content of a song be conveyed to the listener, diction becomes highly important. Teachers often appoint several children to evaluate tone quality and diction. These children may listen as the class sings and report their findings, which can lead to improvement of the rendition of the song. The study of interpretive expression is an integral part of this procedure, and terms such as *crescendo, diminuendo,* and

---

[1] Satis N. Coleman, *Creative Music for Children* (New York: G. P. Putnam's Sons, 1922).

accent have genuine meaning because they are an integral part of children's efforts to convey meaning through the singing of songs.

In order to teach singing properly, the teacher needs a knowledge of the child's voice generally and on various grade levels specifically. The range of problems is very wide—from the beginning of the first-grade year when less than half of the children are normally able to match tones, to the sixth-grade year when some of the boys' voices are in the preliminary stages of change. Some of the research bearing on the child voice will be reported in later chapters. It seems fair to state that although existing knowledge of this subject is very helpful, more research is needed to resolve fully some of the conflicting ideas concerning the pitch range of the average voice at different age levels, the amount of normal deviation that exists, and the means of providing for such individual differences.

Part-singing, once an activity confined to Grades 4, 5, and 6, has been included in the lower grades through the use of simple chants, descants, and rounds. Certain instrumental parts to be played along with the melody in primary grades songs can first be played on keyboard instruments by children, then sung by those who are ready for simple part-singing activities. True part-singing remains essentially an intermediate grades activity although an occasional third grade is capable of it.

Note-reading is a normal activity in any organized music program. Notation is a visual image of the pitch and duration of the tones heard; thus it constitutes a picture or illustration that assists music understanding. It is obviously useful in making music by instrument or voice. Reasonable comprehension of notation enables the learner to advance far beyond the confines of simple rote learning.

Today, note-reading seems to be experiencing a revival of interest after a marked decline in the 1940's and early 1950's. This decline may have occurred for several reasons: (1) the earlier overemphasis on note-reading prompted a reaction against the teaching of much notation; (2) the entry into music teaching of a large group of classroom teachers who had little understanding of note-reading prevented its being taught adequately; and (3) insufficient knowledge of the learning process led to an overemphasis on rote learning and recreational activities.

Although education today would look askance at attempts to subject children to isolated drills intended to foster the learning of notation, it is interesting to note the number of suggestions for relating songs and rhythm activities to notation which are to be found in recent books for the first grade. Both the *Birchard Series: Book One* and *This Is Music: Book One* introduce notation to the children in several ways. This is a far cry from the 1940's, when in many schools references to notation were delayed until the fourth or fifth grade.

As in the teaching of other aspects of the curriculum, such concepts of learning as readiness, provision for individual differences, practice, and continuity should be brought into play in the teaching of note-reading. Two guiding principles have been asserted to be: "(1) that learning music notation should be an integral part of the various music activities of the music program rather than something taught in isolation, and (2) that notation should be taught in a way that serves an immediately useful or interesting purpose to children." [2]

The old question of whether to use the Latin syllables, numerals, letter names, or combinations of these still persists. It is probably best answered by advising the questioner to employ the device by which he can achieve the greatest success in terms of the children's ability to use notation. With the use of the keyboard—cardboard replicas, the piano, bell sets, xylophones—note names can be used and learned quickly. However, certain ear training activities that enable the listener to "see" in notation the pitches he hears seem to require syllables or numerals.

The Latin syllables are excellent from the vocal standpoint; numerals are not as musical, and scale-tone "seven" contains one too many word syllables to be rhythmically correct. (Some teachers omit the second syllable.) Syllables are meaningless and do not relate directly to chords and intervals in music theory, while numerals are familiar terminology and are applicable. But it is practically impossible to sing chromatic music with numerals, while the syllables will accommodate it. Children, however, do not like either device very well: they want to sing words! Numerals and syllables should be used in the solution of music problems in ear training or in reading notation, never in drill activities that are without mean-

---

[2] Robert E. Nye and Vernice T. Nye, *Music in the Elementary School* (Englewood Cliffs, N.J.: Prentice-Hall, Inc., 1957), p. 177.

ing or purpose to children. Furthermore, the instrumentalist can learn to read music by letter names without using either syllables or numerals. Since recent music series books abound with opportunities for children to use notation instrumentally as well as vocally, and commonly employ numerals, syllables, and letter names, teachers have the opportunity to teach notation in a number of different ways.[3] Actually, it should be taught in relation to all other activities in the complete music program.

Listening is a basic music activity. Unless children listen carefully to pitches, they cannot imitate them accurately. Unless they listen critically to the musical performance of their class, they will not discover ways to improve this performance. If they have not learned to listen for harmonic changes, melodic contours, rhythm patterns, form, dynamics, instrumentation, and other aspects of music, they remain relatively untouched by music and can never gain a genuine understanding of it. Listening is therefore, perhaps the most important music activity, and every music period should contain numerous opportunities to listen so that exploration and discovery in the vast world of musical sound can take place.

Listening to recordings is a part of the program of listening experiences. In the primary grades, the teacher's major objectives are to teach the children to respond to recorded music physically and emotionally and to identify instruments. In the intermediate grades these objectives are gradually expanded to include a greater degree of intellectual response. For example, the child in the primary grades will listen to determine whether the music sounds happy or sad, fast or slow, loud or soft, calm or stormy, or if it tells a story. Frequently some of these simple responses will be expressed in bodily movement. The child in the intermediate grades should determine these same things, and bodily movement can have a place here also. He will also "feel" the emotional response and define it, or find the story if there is one. After this should come the intellectual response to questions posed by the teacher concerning *how* the music conveys the feeling or story. The musical means that convey these impressions may include melody, rhythm, harmony, instrumentation, dynamics, form, melodic and rhythmic patterns, and tempo. Concepts

---

[3] Still another system for teaching understanding of notation is described in W. Otto Miessner, "The Art of Tonal Thinking," *Music Educators Journal* (January, 1962), 42-45.

of the different instruments are greatly enhanced by determining the particular quality of an instrument that led to its selection by the composer or arranger to achieve a particular effect.

Another aspect of the listening program is knowledge about some of the great composers. This is secondary, however, to the study of the music itself. It is most effective when the children have so enjoyed the music that they are genuinely interested in the person who created it. Teachers collect anecdotes about composers to "humanize" them for the children, especially those anecdotes that concern children or that concern the composer as a child.

In order to teach listening activities well, the teacher must possess sufficient musical background to be able to analyze the music thoroughly. Unless he possesses this ability, he will be unable to plan questions that will motivate and stimulate learning in this important part of the music program.

Rhythmic responses have been an important aspect of the music program, particularly since the early twentieth century work of Emil Jaques-Dalcroze, a Swiss musician whose experiments in interpreting music through large bodily movements revealed such movement as a foundation stone in teaching musical understanding. American music educators have adapted and simplified the rather complex system of Dalcroze to suit their own purposes. Some of their applications are found in music series books, often expressing aspects of notation through movement. With the growth in knowledge about the needs of growing children has come increasing acceptance of action songs, singing games, and dances—not only in the music period, but at any time of the day when they are needed for resting, for relaxing, and for stemming fatigue.

One development, the rhythm band, is exceedingly popular—particularly at first- and second-grade levels. For some years these "bands" were formed as replicas of adult bands, with the teacher dictating, from a published score, every move of the players of little percussion instruments. In later years this use of percussion instruments became much more creative, and the published score is now seldom seen. In today's schools, these instruments are used in every grade for various purposes—sometimes to emphasize the feeling of rhythm, sometimes to teach aspects of notation, and very often to add aesthetically satisfying sound effects that enhance the song or activity.

Creative dramatizations and creative adaptations of singing games, action songs, and dances are part of the music curriculum of today.

Playing simple instruments has been a growing aspect of the music curriculum for some years. Besides the percussion instruments mentioned above, there are keyboard instruments and small wind instruments. The keyboard constitutes a very significant audio-visual tool in the teaching of pitch and notation concepts, and it can be used also in the teaching of part-singing. On the piano keyboard and on the keyboard of the bell sets and xylophones, the learner can see, hear, and feel whole steps, half-steps, chords, intervals, sharps, flats, and other music "fundamentals" that might otherwise remain mysteries in a shadowy world of unexplained sound. For this reason, the modern music series book contains keyboard experiences. In the intermediate grades full-fledged piano chording is developed. This is a strong step toward a basic understanding of simple music theory. Furthermore, it is a simple skill that has recreational and creative values throughout life.

The simple wind instruments include the recorder, recorder-type instruments, and flute-type instruments. In the general music program, it is assumed that every child needs some experience playing such an instrument. Such instruments are particularly useful in teaching an understanding of music notation in a genuinely functional setting. They can assist part-singing when they play descant parts or vocal parts other than the melody.

Creative activities are not detached from the other activities of the curriculum: a creative approach should permeate every activity. It has been said that creativity in the classroom is not apt to occur without background, skills, a variety of materials, freedom to explore, and unobtrusive guidance from the teacher. It has also been said that creativity is something that permeates a classroom and frees the student to do independent thinking rather than being confined to a specific activity. When children study a song to improve its interpretation, their trial-and-error procedure is assumed to have many creative aspects, for creativity is a problem-solving process in which play and work become one. Dramatization and rhythmic responses can be creative; vocal or instrumental parts can be improvised and added to the score; "new" movements can be added to a patterned dance; dances can be invented; songs can be created;

sound effects can be added; introductions and codas can be invented, and even little operettas can be put together with speaking parts, songs from the books, and songs created for the situation.

Possibilities for creative activities abound in music. Research indicates that the creative outlook is transferrable to other activities; that is, once a child has learned to be creative in music, he is very likely to be creative in many other activities. Teachers who have learned to be creative themselves are most apt to help children approach the problems of contemporary living in the creative manner that seems essential to the continuance of our civilization.

Interrelationships with other areas does not necessarily imply music activities as such, but comprises certain opportunities a teacher has to enhance the musical subject matter at hand. Music and certain other areas relate very well. From the standpoint of the objectives of the music program, this relation will assist in the teaching of music, and contribute to the children's learning of music in some way.

However, music is often used to assist nonmusical objectives in other areas. Whether or not the children are learning about music at the same time music is serving nonmusical purposes would have to be subject to analysis. Since music is an important part of world culture, it assumes great importance in leading to an understanding of the various peoples of the world and thus is indispensible in teaching the social studies. It serves physical education. It relates to science and mathematics. It is a communicative art, and as such relates to the language arts program. Its utility and versatility are unique. However, the teacher must be able to differentiate between the teaching of music and the use of music as a tool to assist learning in other areas.

Today's curriculum is much more complex than that of the early years of this century and much more demanding in terms of the preparation of the teacher. The following chart,[4] prepared by the Oregon State Department of Education, divides basic music activities into three categories: listening to music, moving to music, and making music by singing and playing. It shows for what broad educational purposes the teacher is to guide children in these activities.

---

[4] *Music Education in Oregon Public Schools* (Salem, Oregon: State Department of Education, 1960), p. 4.

SCOPE AND SEQUENCE OF THE SCHOOL MUSIC PROGRAM

Each of these
MUSIC EXPERIENCES

Listen to Music	(in many instances **COULD** do all of these)	Give Pleasure
Moving to Music		Develop Music Skills
		Develop Creative Capacities
Making Music by	(in the aggregate **SHOULD** ultimately do all of these)	Develop Knowledge of Music Literature
Singing		Develop Understanding of the Symbols and Vocabulary of Music
Playing		
		Develop Understanding of the Structure of Music
	(in specific cases **MAY** do part only, of these)	Develop Understanding of Human Feelings and Their Expression

Fifty years ago the music teacher was often called "the singing teacher." Today it is unlikely that any teacher who organizes a balanced program of music instruction will be called "the singing teacher" because there are now many activities other than singing in such a program. However, singing is still considered to be the most important single activity by most music educators. The most important comment about the present music education curriculum is that with so many varied activities there is a place for every boy and girl to achieve success in some aspect of music.

It is well to remember the recommendations of the 1960 White House Conference on Children and Youth: that the school curriculum should contain "instruction in our own diversified culture and the cultures of other peoples through such disciplines as literature, social sciences, art, and music," and that there should also be "an expanded program in music and art to encourage creativity." [5]

A sequential development of the music program. The remainder of this chapter consists of a portion of the *Bethel Music Curriculum: A Scope and Sequence of Musical Experiences for Boys and*

[5] *Implications for Elementary Education:* Followup on the 1960 White House Conference on Children and Youth, U.S. Office of Education Circular, OE-20033 (Washington, D.C.: USGPO, 1961), p. 4.

Girls, Volume I.[6] It is the result of the study and experience of an elementary school music staff, working together to plan an improved music program for Grades 1–6. Although some of its aspects, such as "Dance steps, skills and formations" in Grades 1 and 2 are in advance of accepted practice, it is a good example of planned sequential development based upon a music series.

SPECIFIC PROCEDURES FOR IMPLEMENTING A SEQUENTIAL DEVELOPMENT OF THE MUSIC PROGRAM AT GRADE LEVEL

These specifics indicate appropriate levels for introducing various concepts. It is to be understood that, once introduced, these concepts will be carried on throughout the program. The teacher should constantly seek varied means of reinforcing ideas that have been presented earlier. Activities introduced in simple form in the primary grades should be continued, developed, and expanded throughout the program to increase ability and understanding.

It is to be understood that this program is based upon sequential development; therefore, the extent to which each group can be introduced to new steps recommended at each grade level depends upon previous experience. Preschool experience, community cultural influences, and family environment will also influence the rate and level of presentation of this program, or at least the degree of understanding which can be developed and the approach for presenting these concepts.

First Grade:

1. Many songs with a compass of a fifth should be used for group singing.

2. Intervals in the songs should be predominantly diatonic.

3. As a rule, the most logical pitch range for group songs will be from for songs with a compass of a fifth and from

     for those with a compass of an octave.

4. Because of a wide variation of size and placement of children's voice ranges, it will be necessary to include a considerable amount of individual singing to accommodate individual

---

[6] A publication of the Bethel School District Number 52, Eugene, Oregon.

differences and provide successful singing experiences for all
children.

5. Opportunities for individual singing can be provided by:
   a. Informally sung question and answers.
   b. Creative tonal response games. Do not give the child a
      feeling of being pressured to match specific pitches accu-
      rately. Freedom in singing should come first. Match the
      child's pitch and encourage him to sing from this starting
      point. Never create situations where the child is left with
      a feeling of failure.
   c. Individual singing of short phrases in a song that the
      group is singing.
   d. Encouraging those who wish to sing whole songs for the
      class.

6. Ear-training for specific intervals should concentrate within a
   compass of a fifth. Physical and visual experiences should
   accompany the presentations of these pitch relationships.
   a. Help children learn to discriminate between highs and
      lows in pitch by:
      (1) Using hands to illustrate highs and lows in the songs
          they sing.
      (2) Discussing and responding physically to high and
          low sounds in recorded music.
      (3) Illustrating on song bells held in an upright position.
      (4) Experimenting with melodic instruments.
      (5) In order to provide a visual means whereby the child
          can better understand high and low as well as dura-
          tion it is helpful to use this technique: Take a piece
          of chalk and use the side of it as you also show
          duration, writing simple patterns ▬ ▬
                                               ▬ ▬

          Then make the transfer to notation.

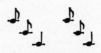

   b. Guide children in learning to discriminate the direction
      of melodic movement (e.g., up, down, or in the same
      place). Opportunities for developing this can be pro-
      vided by:
      (1) Using hand or body motions to illustrate the direc-
          tion of the melodic line as they listen to songs or
          recordings or as they sing.
      (2) Playing, observing, and listening to the direction that
          the melody moves on the song bells. (Holding the

instrument in an upright position will help clarify this concept.)

(3) Observing the pattern of the melody in notation and illustrating the pattern of the melody by lines on the blackboard.

c. When the direction of melodic movement is established, children should be guided in discovering that music moves up or down by steps and skips. Further experiences with the song bells and identification of steps and skips in songs will develop increased discrimination in identifying melodic movement.

d. When children can hear and identify steps and skips in the music, numbers can be introduced. Because of the number concepts developed through use of the Stern's materials in the first grade, these children will be able to make a rapid transfer of steps and skips to number relationships. (*e.g.,* When they have identified a pattern as step, step, step, step, step going up, teacher can say, "If this is one what does the pattern say?" They will be able to tell that it says 1-2-3-4-5.) Once this transfer is made, children will be able to identify the numbers for the melodic pattern of simple songs, write the pattern on the board, and play it on the songbells. They can also do the same for songs they create. It is usually better to do this as a group project with the teacher writing on the board because the small muscle coordination is not well developed at this age thus writing is slow and tedious.

e. When these pitch relationships are developed, the children can be guided to discover how music is notated. Observation of melodic movement of songs written on large charts should precede this experience. A flannel board or magnaboard is useful for presenting this concept because they are easier for children to manipulate than writing on the board. Explain that music is written on a staff with five lines and four spaces between. Ask children if they know how we would write music that says 1-2-3, placing 1 on the staff. Someone will discover the correct way after discussion of what it should look like. Once children learn that steps move from line to space to line, and skips from line to line or space to space, and that 1 can be placed in different locations, they can read and write music that encompasses intervals that they have been trained to hear and reproduce. Notating their own music as a class, notating phrases of songs on the magnaboard, reading songs from charts, playing them on songbells, and notating intervals on the magnaboard will develop further skill.

7. Physical rhythmic skills that should be explored and developed are:

   a. Basic locomotor movements. These should be explored in relation to concepts of space, directions, level of movement, intensity, and variations of tempo.

     (1) Walk
     (2) Run
     (3) Jump
     (4) Hop
     (5) Skip
     (6) Combined patterns of walk, run, and long bow.

   b. Non-locomotor movements

     (1) Swing
     (2) Bend
     (3) Twist
     (4) Rock or sway
     (5) Stretch
     (6) Push
     (7) Pull

   c. Dance steps, skills and formations:

     (1) Gallop
     (2) Slide
     (3) Skip
     (4) Step hop
     (5) Rock or balance
     (6) Bow to partner
     (7) Bow to neighbor
     (8) Circle
     (9) Single circle with partner on the right
    (10) Double circle
    (11) Double circle with partners side by side
    (12) Double circle facing partner
    (13) Two hands around
    (14) Long way set
    (15) Sashay
    (16) Right and left elbow swing
    (17) Triple circle
    (18) Move on to next partner
    (19) Line of direction
    (20) Opposite line of direction

8. Specific rhythmic notation and relationship to be presented are ♩ 𝄾 ♪ , 𝅗𝅥 . All such presentations should be an outgrowth of active exploration of rhythmic movement.

a. These relationships should be developed in terms of basic movement: $\quad \downarrow \, \xi$ = walk, $\quad \downarrow \, \gamma$ = run, and $\quad \downarrow$ = long bow.

b. When children can execute the basic movements in response to percussive and instrumental accompaniment and can hear, identify, step and play these rhythms, the printed symbol can be introduced.

c. Further skill can be developed by notating rhythmic patterns of the songs they sing and create, and by reading rhythmic patterns for singing, playing instruments and stepping patterns.

d. Because of the problem of muscular coordination, the children at this level will be unable to notate rhythms rapidly on the board. To facilitate notating rhythms, notes can be made on 5 x 8 cards and the children can select the correct note and place the cards along the chalkboard to illustrate the rhythmic notation.

9. A feeling for the basic beat should be developed through physical response and use of percussive instruments. The children should be able to determine whether music moves in 2's, 3's, or 4's.

10. Tempo changes, dynamics, intensity, and accents should be experienced through physical response such as:
    a. Clapping.
    b. Stepping.
    c. Creative rhythmic dramatization of songs and recorded music.
    d. Creating suitable accompaniments with percussive, melodic and chordal instruments. (Providing experience with a wide variety of tempo and dynamic changes will help increase awareness and response of children to these elements.)

11. An awareness of mood, movement, and emotional content of music can be developed by:
    a. Helping children listen to the way music moves (*e.g.*, smooth or sharp, short or snappy, or rolling and drifting).
    b. Helping children describe their reaction to music through descriptive adjectives.
    c. Helping the class plan their interpretation of song in terms of feeling, mood and tempo.
    d. Freely discussing recorded music in terms of how it moves and how it makes you feel.
    e. Providing opportunity for creative movement to music to demonstrate and apply these concepts individually.

12. An awareness of harmony can be developed by:
    a. Singing simple descants and rounds.

b. Exploring combinations of sounds on melodic instruments.
c. Following chord changes of I, IV, and V on the autoharp.
d. Playing chords on autoharp and resonator bells to accompany songs.

13. An awareness of form can be developed by:
a. Moving arms in circle to the phrases of the songs they sing.
b. Having different groups move to each phrase of the music.
c. Creative movement to question and answer phrasing in music.
d. Guiding children to recognize phrasing as a musical idea, similar to a sentence in speaking.
e. Application and recognition of phrasing in creative efforts.
f. Developing awareness of contrasting sections in music through creative movement and instrumental accompaniments to recorded music.
g. When awareness of contrasts is established, children can begin recognizing and identifying the pattern of simple forms (*e.g.,* ABA, ABACA, etc.).

14. Rhythm instruments.
a. Rhythm instruments should be introduced separately.
b. Children should consider these as instruments for creating music and not as toys.
c. Proper care, use, and technique of playing each instrument should be taught.
d. Standards for using, distributing and taking up instruments should be developed.
e. Each child should have an opportunity to experiment with the quality of sound that can be produced on each instrument.
f. Discrimination in the use of the instruments for interpreting music should be developed.
   (1) Guide children in creating suitable accompaniments for the songs they sing.
   (2) Guide children in planning their own instrumentation for accompanying recorded selections.
   (3) Children should become aware of the suitability of the quality and intensity of sound that should be used in relation to the mood, dynamics, and emotional content of the music.
   (4) As skill in the use of the instrument is developed, children can combine creative movement with their instrumental accompaniment to dramatize what they hear in the music.

15. Develop standards for listening to music by guiding discussion of the following points:
    a. Why we listen quietly to music . . . music is sound.
    b. What we listen for.
    c. Respect for other listeners.
    d. Respect for performers.
16. Selections for listening at this age level should be short with clearly marked characteristics such as:
    a. Music that is highly rhythmic.
    b. Music that suggests mood or emotion.
    c. Music that tells a story or is descriptive.
17. With awareness of what is happening in other areas in the classroom, the music teacher can correlate music to enrich the other classroom experiences. Correlation at this level will be limited primarily to the topical selection of songs, rhythms and creative material related to the units taught such as the farm, circus or special holidays.
18. Creative experiences that should be provided are:
    a. Opportunities for self-expression through music by singing conversations as a free form of response with no thought of preserving the melody.
    b. Making up words for a song.
    c. Creating own songs as a group.
    d. Creating steps and dances in response to music without the stress of developing set formal patterns.
    e. Creating instrumental accompaniments to songs and recorded music.
    f. Creating rhythmic movements for songs (*e.g.,* Punchinello, Adam Had 7 Sons).
    g. Dramatizing songs, song stories, and recorded music that tells a story.
    h. Free creative movement to recorded music.
    i. Having opportunities to discuss appropriate tone quality, volume and tempo for interpreting songs in relation to the mood, purpose and style of the music.
19. Skills that should be developed in interpreting music through body movement are:
    a. Responding to the emotional quality of the music through posture and facial expression.
    b. Awareness of use of space.
    c. Awareness of use of levels of movement.
    d. Use of various directions of movement.
    e. Use of all parts of the body in free response to the flow of the music. Encourage the children to feel that the music flows in their ears and then to the tips of the fingers, toes, and head and comes out in movement.

20. Musical terms that should be defined are:
    a. Staff
    b. Barline
    c. Double bar
    d. G clef
    e. Repeat sign
    f. P. (piano)
    g. Mezzo (medium)
    h. Ritard
    i. A tempo
    j. Melody
    k. Harmony
    l. Tempo
    m. Volume
    n. Rhythm
    o. Accent

Second Grade:

1. Group songs can include more songs with a compass of an octave.
2. Individual singing will no longer be as necessary for providing for individual differences but should be encouraged for developing independence in singing.
3. Opportunities for developing independence in singing can be provided by:
    a. Singing informal conversations.
    b. Having individuals sing the verse of a song and the class the chorus.
    c. Having children teach a song to the class.
    d. Encouraging children to make up their own songs and sing them to the class.
    e. Having children make up and sing additional verses to songs they already know.
    f. Singing rounds and descants and having individuals lead each section.
    g. Encouraging children to sing whole songs for the class.
4. Ear-training for specific intervals can be expanded to encompass the octave with similar experiences provided for furthering ear-training, reading, and notating skill as in the first grade.
5. Much board and chart work is still advisable at this level, so that attention of the children may be centered.
6. Music books can be introduced. Children should be guided in transferring pitch relationships that have been developed aurally to the printed symbols. As their interval vocabulary increases and is associated with the printed symbol, inde-

pendent reading ability will develop. It should be remembered that reading words is still difficult for second graders.

7. Experiences should be provided for developing individual independence in notating music.
   a. Notating songs on the board, having different individuals write each measure.
   b. Notating songs they have created.
   c. Building note patterns at their desks from dictation. Cardboard staffs or those found in the back of their music books are useful for this purpose. Children can use cutout tag board notes to build the tonal patterns. In this way the teacher can identify and assist individuals that need help.

8. Terms to be defined:
   a. Measure
   b. Fermata
   c. D. C. al fine

9. Develop understanding that chords in a scale pattern are built on skips. Find I, IV, V chords on resonator bells.

10. Provide a variety of visual experiences in writing and building chords.

11. Understanding of the rhythmic relationship of ♩ ♩. ♫ ♩ should be developed.

12. An understanding of the top number in the time signature can be developed in relation to their experience of how music moves and the feeling for the basic beat in 2's, 3's, 4's, and 6's.

13. As independence in reading rhythmic patterns develops and as the children are able to associate rhythmic notation and relationships at sight, melody and rhythm can be read simultaneously.

14. Further understanding of harmony can be developed by:
   a. Singing simple descants, rounds, and simple harmonization.
   b. Developing understanding of the term *harmony* as the combining of pitches, and exploring the added color that it gives to music.
   c. Developing the ability to chord I, IV, and V accompaniments on the autoharp independently.

15. Develop further understanding of form by including pattern music with interludes and codas and more complicated patterns.

16. Develop understanding of how folk music is a natural expression which reflects the characteristics of the country and the way people live, feel, and work.

17. Become acquainted with family groupings of familiar orchestra instruments.
18. Dramatize stories in instrumental music to develop more discrimination in response to tempo and dynamics and in use of levels of movement.
19. Combine movement and instrumentation.
20. Develop greater awareness of use of space in relationship to movements of others.
21. Add to vocabulary of rhythmic skills:
    a. Form a square
    b. Do-si-do
    c. Partner and corner
    d. Promenade
    e. Circle four, circle eight, and so forth
    f. Head couples and side couples
    g. Balance
    h. Bleking step

Third Grade:
1. Due to expanded ranges, it will be possible to include songs with a wider compass for group singing.
2. Harmony, rounds, and descants will furnish the primary means of accommodating individual differences in voice range.
3. Opportunities for developing independence in singing can be provided by:
    a. An extension of suggestion for second grade.
    b. Planning formal room programs.
4. Children will usually begin experiencing a more definite need for choral and vocal techniques.
5. Develop ability to improvise own harmony part.
6. Continue to experiment with chord-building, using the resonator bells.
7. Develop awareness of composers' use of harmony in descriptive music.
8. Pitch relationships above and below the octave can be introduced for ear-training and independent reading.
9. Children will become more independent in reading music from books but will still profit from preparatory activities centered on board or chart.
10. Begin associating musical names for rhythmic notation but continue to use both terms (quarter = walk, eighth = run, and so forth).
11. Children can begin taking dictation of intervals and simple melodies as well as writing their own melodies on staff paper.
12. Understanding of the rhythmic relationship of ♩. ♪ | ♫

should be developed. Meaning of dotted rhythms at this level should be represented in terms of adding to the length of the note and in relation to the rhythm of the skip.

13. Begin a transfer of rhythmic values from movement response and relationship to numerical time values. Discover in terms of the basic beat that if a walk is 1, ♩ gets 2 beats, ♩. gets 3 beats, ○ gets 4 beats and that it takes ♫ to make one beat. Provide concrete experiences in clapping, playing, and stepping ♪ to ♩ , ♩ to ♩, and so forth, and in playing, singing, and stepping rhythmic patterns of music above the basic beat.

14. Apply knowledge of form in creative songs.

15. Introduce longer forms in music through descriptive music, and develop awareness of difference between this and pattern music through creative rhythmic dramatization.

16. Demonstrate and experiment with the scientific principles of tone production of various instruments of the orchestra.
    a. Provide opportunities for seeing and hearing "live" instruments whenever possible, in addition to recorded demonstrations.
    b. Encourage children to make instruments.
    c. Provide visual demonstrations of scientific principles of tone production.

17. Develop awareness of the composer's use of instrumental tone color, volume, rhythm, melody, and tempo in compositions.

18. Correlate subject matter of songs and rhythms materials with classroom activities whenever possible.

19. Children should create their own pattern dances.

20. Add to rhythms vocabulary:
    a. Right-hand star, left-hand star
    b. Grand right and left
    c. Heel-toe
    d. Polka
    e. Two-step
    f. Reel
    g. Allemande left and right
    h. Ladies' chain

21. Terms to be defined:
    a. Quarter-note
    b. Eighth-note
    c. Half-note
    d. Whole note
    e. Sixteenth-note
    f. Poco rit.
    g. Accent >

h. D. S. (dal segno)
i. Crescendo <
j. Decrescendo >
k. mp
l. Grace note ♪
m. Canon

Fourth Grade:

1. Individual differences in voice range and ability can be provided for by increased use of part singing, descants, and individual singing.
2. The teacher will need to know the vocal capabilities, background, and experience of each child. Song material should be carefully selected to provide for individual differences and also take into consideration the interest and maturity level of the group. By fourth grade it becomes increasingly important to select song material that has appeal for boys in order to maintain a high level of participation and interest in group singing.
3. Technical understanding of pitch relationships in major and minor tonalities can be developed. Understanding of patterns in steps and half-steps should grow out of experimentation on melodic instruments.
4. Experiences should be provided in singing and identifying major and minor chords. Minor chords should be used in autoharp or bell accompaniments.
5. Ear-training to develop the ability to identify and reproduce the more difficult intervals of 4th, 6th, and 7th can be emphasized. Children at this age level enjoy short drills in interval recognition if conducted as contests or games.
6. By relating the more difficult skips in music (*e.g.,* 2, 4, 6) to chordal concepts, reading will be facilitated.
7. Experiences with the keyboard, song bells, and resonator bells should lead to an understanding of the purpose of the key signature and the reason for flatting or sharping notes in different keys.
8. Knowledge of pitch names and how to find 1 in any key can be an outgrowth of this experience.
9. Explanation of the G-clef sign may be presented at this time.
10. Children should understand and have experience using conductor's beat for 2's, 3's, and 4's.
11. Children should be introduced to longer forms in music: symphonic poem, suite, dance forms, opera, overture, aria, recitative, operetta, fugue, theme, and variation.
12. Understanding of composer's use of form should be developed through discussion of the music that the children hear.

13. Terminology for types of pattern music may be introduced: Two parts, three parts, rondo.
14. The following should be added to the repertoire of rhythmic skills:
    a. Waltz-balance
    b. Waltz
    c. Two-step
    d. Three-step
    e. Schottische
    f. Grapevine step
15. Terms to be defined:
    a. First and second ending
    b. Syncopated ryhthm
    c. Triplets
    d. Common time
    e. "Cut" time (alla breve)

Fifth Grade:

1. At this stage of development some boys may begin losing the upper notes in their singing range. The teacher will need to know each child's vocal problems and limitations, and will assign part sections when advisable. Children with flexible ranges can be shifted from section to section, but no child should be expected to sing in a range that is not comfortable or within his ability.
2. Ear-training should be directed toward singing and hearing pitch relationships in chordal sequences (*e.g.,* singing a major chord and lowering the third to change it to minor, singing and playing simple chord sequences, and listening for voice movement and change of pitch relationships.)
3. An understanding of the lower numbers of the key signature may now be developed in terms of fractional relationships. This should not be done until children have worked with fractions in arithmetic. Visual aids (fractions on flannel board, rhythmic patterns on board demonstrating fractional relationships) should be used to develop understanding.
4. Further independence in reading more complicated rhythmic patterns should be developed.
5. Develop further understanding of numerical value of notes in terms of the time signature and through experiences listed in 3.
6. As understanding develops, notes can be referred to by musical name. Refer back to movement equivalent when difficulty is encountered in feeling the rhythm.
7. Modern jazz rhythms should be explored through movement and use of percussive instruments.

8. Ability to read and understand syncopated rhythms may be developed as an outgrowth of the above, and in connection with the study of American music.
9. Conductors' pattern for 6's should be introduced.
10. Experiences should be provided in chord-building, singing, and playing all chords in different keys.
11. Awareness of basic chord structure in accompaniments and harmony should be developed.
12. Children should become aware of difference between polyphonic and harmonic structure.
13. Children should gain an overall view of the development of music in America including: sea chanteys, music of the colonies, patriotic songs and songs of the Armed Forces, music and dances connected with the westward movement, Negro spirituals and revival tunes, development of jazz, musical comedy in America, American composers and performing artists.
14. Understanding should be developed of the interaction of cultural and historical factors in the development of American music.
15. Experimentation with pentatonic and modal scale patterns may be an outgrowth of the study of American music.
16. Children should become aware of types of form employed for various kinds of music studied: folklore music, popular music, art music, vocal, instrumental, and theater music. Understanding should be developed as to the influence of the purpose of the music on its form.
17. American dances should be presented in relation to the cultural influences of their period.
18. Push step and buzz step should be added to the rhythmic repertoire.
19. Terms to be defined:
    a. Andante
    b. Allegro
    c. Diminuendo

Sixth Grade:

1. Increased use of three-part music will facilitate providing for individual differences.
2. At this level it is necessary to observe carefully, retest individuals frequently, and reassign parts, especially for boys' voices.
3. Toward the latter half of the year many of the boys' voices will begin to change. Singing experiences may be provided for these children by allowing them to sing an octave below the melody, if the range of the song is not too extreme. They

may also use a chord base (I, IV, V, using the root of the chord) for their part.

4. Because of the social, physical, and emotional changes occurring at this grade level, it will be necessary to use great care in the selection of materials in order to provide challenging and successful experiences and still maintain a high level of interest and participation.

5. Introduction of vocal techniques can usually be approached in a more technical manner as understanding of need and purpose is developed.

6. Discussion of voice classifications and the changing voice is important so that the children understand the changes that are occurring in their singing voices.

7. Skills in ear-training, reading, and notating should be reviewed and evaluated, with concentration on areas of weakness.

8. Rhythmic skills should be reviewed in the same manner.

9. Children should develop awareness of harmonic structure in three-part singing.

10. Further experiences should be provided in singing and playing chord sequences.

11. Children should develop ability to write chord sequences in different keys.

12. Opportunity should be provided for harmonizing and working out accompaniments to creative efforts.

13. A general understanding of Mexican and South American music should be developed together with the cultural and historical factors which influenced its development.

14. Understanding should be developed of polyrhythmic music, syncopation, and music with a changing accent, such as 5/4 and 7/4 time, in relation to the characteristics of Latin American music.

15. Latin American rhythms should be explored through use of movement and percussive instruments.

16. Further understanding of form can be developed through analysis of forms used in the music of Latin America, and comparison with music of our country. This should lead to an awareness of factors influencing composers' selection of form in their compositions.

17. Mexican and Latin American folk dances should be presented in relation to the cultural factors which influenced their development.

18. Children should become familiar with Latin American instruments: bongo, claves, castanets, tambourine, guiro. Experience with these instruments should lead to an awareness of the effect of instrumentation on music.

19. Mexican and South American dance steps should be added to the rhythmic repertoire.
20. Choral experience should be provided for the more gifted children at this level if possible.
21. Terms to be defined:
    a. Con spirito
    b. Misterioso
    c. Allegretto
    d. Spiritoso
    e. Poco a poco
    f. Barcarolle
    g. Waltz tempo
    h. March tempo
    i. Tarantella
    j. Maestoso
    k. Andantino
    l. Rubato
    m. Moderato

CHAPTER III

Music, Child Development, and Learning

Anyone who teaches music effectively must know the child and his developmental characteristics. Education today is more complex than in earlier years when teachers organized music programs around subject matter assumed to be appropriate for each grade level. In the 1940's there appeared an increasing awareness of child development and its effect upon learning in all areas. In music education, teachers began to evaluate the effects of music upon personality and social and emotional growth. Despite the fact that present knowledge and research is incomplete, no one can afford to ignore the data which exist. The teacher needs to know how experiences in music can contribute to the optimum development of each child, and which music experiences will contribute most to this development.

In the elementary school, music is often a means rather than an end in itself. It is a means to the child's understanding of various aspects of music which interest him, and also a means to his understanding of his own behavior, that of his classmates, and that of his local, national, and international community. This does not imply that skills are to be neglected, however. When music skills are acquired in functional relation to pupils' interests, purposes, needs, and abilities, they are not only of greater significance and more quickly learned, but will contribute far more to personality development than a program which emphasizes music skills in isolation from these other aspects.

There is a large amount of research in the general area of child development which teachers need to know and to relate to music teaching. Data concerned specifically with music are meager, and there are dangers in accepting this incomplete body of research without reservations.

Although knowledge of the general characteristics of the various age levels will always be an important tool for teachers, knowledge of the individual differences among children of these age levels and how these can be accommodated has risen to almost equal importance. This has come about because the best education today attempts to assist every child in his efforts to achieve a balanced development, and we have learned that every child is different in some ways from every other child. Thus, today's curriculum must be adaptable and flexible, and today's teaching demands a far greater degree of knowledge and expertness than was necessary in the past.

It was stated that very little research in child development has been done in the area of music education. By comparison, research in art education has revealed specific stages of development through which the child's artistic conceptualizations advance step by step. Unfortunately, the stages of musical development have not yet been similarly defined. Little is known of the learning process in music. Although music teachers have learned much from practical experience, the research which might support some of their beliefs has not yet been conducted. The child voice, music reading, creating and improvising music, and the format of printed music materials are among the areas which are in need of further research.

Research Concerning the Young Child

The accomplishments of Mrs. Satis Coleman [1] and Carl Orff [2] are probably best classified under the heading of "action research." Mrs. Coleman (see p. 10) is a pioneering music educator at Lincoln School, Columbia University. Carl Orff is a distinguished German composer who became interested in trying to determine the type of music which is truly "music for children." Both believed that when music experiences for children begin, speaking, singing, and moving are integrally related, and that speech patterns lead to the evolution of rhythm patterns and these, in turn, lead to the development of melodic patterns. Both saw music as a creative art, and music education as a reflection of the development of music from earliest times to the present day. Since normal development includes the urge to strike things, both educators designed instruments which children could strike or pluck. Both Coleman and Orff realized—

[1] Satis N. Coleman, *Creative Music for Children* (New York: G. P. Putnam's Sons, 1922).

[2] Carl Orff and Gunild Keetman, *Music for Children*, Vol. I (New York: Associated Music Publishers, Inc., 1956).

either through their own experimenting or through research data—
that the descending minor third was the easiest interval for children
to sing; both utilized the pentatonic framework instrumentally and
vocally as a natural one in which children could create music. The
pentatonic idiom was shown to be a superior means to further the
natural development of children in music because (1) it is easy to
sing, because there are no half-steps, (2) chord changes are nonexistent, (3) harsh dissonances are eliminated, and (4) it is easy to
play on the Orff-designed instruments [3] which can be adapted to the
pentatonic scheme by removing the wooden or metal bars which
sound major scale tones 4 and 7.

The employment of the descending minor third interval and the
pentatonic idiom as well as other aspects of the musical development of children was buttressed by studies of primitive music made
by anthropologists and musicologists and the studies made by the
Pillsbury Foundation for Advancement of Music Education.[4] These
studies, which were concerned with children between the ages of
two and six, found the rhythmic chant as created by children to be
an important basis for musical growth, and the natural vocal chant
to be associated with strong rhythmic activity. The Pillsbury Foundation researchers made a large number of observations of these
children, including the following: Music is normally both individual
and social. Children need freedom to develop normally in music;
however, this freedom should be combined with adult help in accordance with the children's readiness and need for such help. Action patterns at this age are brief and are extended by repetition and
variation; repetition tends to develop clearer understanding and
surer control. Some creative group experiences in music were the
result of a concentration and attention span of as long as thirty minutes—powers with which young children are not usually credited.
New experiences are not immediately re-created; there is a time
lapse. Individual differences are in evidence. Dance in some form
goes on continually: movement for movement's sake is an impor-

---

[3] Orff-designed instruments are currently imported by Rhythm Band, Inc., 407-
409 Throckmorton Street, Fort Worth 2, Texas; Educational Music Bureau, 434
South Wabash Ave., Chicago 5, Illinois; and M. Hohner, Inc., Andrews Road,
Hicksville, Long Island, New York.

[4] Gladys E. Moorehead, et al., Music of Young Children, Vols. I, II, IV (Santa
Barbara, Calif.: Pillsbury Foundation for Advancement of Music Education, 1941-
51).

tant characteristic. Although children sing freely when they are moving, they seem instinctively to recognize music and dance as different media. Some aspects of children's music may not be understood by adults. Most of the songs children are taught to sing are quite unlike their own music, which is nonharmonic and plaintive in quality. At this age, the basic use of instruments is rhythmic, not melodic, and the rhythm is of more importance than the choice of instrument. Children need to explore, experiment with, and use sounds made from every possible type of material.

The child's melodic concepts are different from those of adults and cannot be judged according to those standards. All harmony is complicated to him. He is primarily interested in sounds for their own sake, not in musical story-telling. He needs to hear not only music of our culture, but also the music of many Oriental and primitive peoples. His first technical questions are acoustical, developing from curiosity about what makes sounds. He is able to identify pictures of instruments and to discriminate between sounds of oboe, clarinet, English horn, and bass clarinet at the age of four and a half. At this age he can identify songs from their rhythm without hearing the melody. Before he is five he organizes performing groups, where he can solve such problems as balance and effective combinations of percussion instruments. He learns to select instruments for specific purposes. His own music contains many of the techniques found in adult composition, such as rhythmic variation, sequence, rhythmic counterpoint, augmentation and diminution, antiphony, recurring refrains, and rondo form. Enforced conformity with adult musical ideas is apt to hinder the growth of important musical conceptual patterns and discourage interest in music of more experimental qualities such as some of the contemporary music to which many adults are indifferent today. His musical environment must be full and varied and must possess quality, such as the best in tone-producing and reproducing instruments. Rhythm bands are essentially wrong; the instruments are inadequate and the band restricts and inhibits the child's natural rhythmic flow. Music must be first felt and expressed by the body, then transformed into sound. Teaching has a place, for some musical facts cannot be learned efficiently and economically through experimentation and creative play, but technical training must not be in advance of the child's needs. There must be a balance between creativity and technical training: the child has need of both, and either will suffer without the other, for he has technical needs as his musical growth continues to unfold.

The study warns against attempts to "integrate" music by having children of this age make up songs about other subject matter, or by relating these subjects to similar songs. Music is something the child lives and makes—it is an integral part of his life which is not achieved through any synthetic union with something else. "If music is to be a language for children, they must not only hear it, but make it their own through constant use."[5]

The studies of young children by Jersild and Bienstock suggest that when teachers work with children in motor rhythms, this work should not be centered primarily upon developing in the child the ability to keep perfect time, but rather to give him freedom to improvise his own patterns and to cultivate his general interest in physical response to rhythmical stimuli.[6] They found that the singing range of most four-year-old children was 13 semitones; the five-year-old's range was 17; the six- and seven-year-old's was 22; and the eight-year-old's was 24. According to their research, many teachers today are underestimating the natural range of the child voice, which at the third-grade level is a full two octaves, and only slightly less than that at the first- and second-grade level. Thus, the teacher of music should seek to free the child to develop his natural range.

A more recent study made by William Kirkpatrick [7] with children of five and six years of age stresses the importance of good musical training at home and in school during early childhood. The television and the phonograph were found to be of negligible influence. The greatest influence on the singing ability of children was found in mothers who sang to and with their children, parents who assisted their children in singing, conversations in song, and an active musical environment with singing, instrument-playing and parents with good musical backgrounds. This study found children singing songs a diminished fifth lower than such songs are pitched in school song

[5] Gladys E. Moorehead, *et al.*, *op. cit.*, Vol. IV, p. 27.

[6] Arthur T. Jersild and Sylvia F. Bienstock, *Development of Rhythm in Young Children* (New York: Bureau of Publications, Teachers College, Columbia University, 1935), pp. 95-96.

[7] William Coy Kirkpatrick, Jr., "Relationships Between the Singing Ability of Prekindergarten Children and Their Home Musical Environment" (Doctoral dissertation presented at the University of Southern California, 1958).

books. The U.S. Office of Education is currently supporting a five-year study—"The Development of Auditory Perception of Musical Sounds by Children in the First Six Grades"—administered by Professor Robert G. Petzold, School of Music, University of Wisconsin. This study is scheduled for completion by July 31, 1965. Among a number of its early implications is the following:

> The existence, within each grade level, of children with marked differences in terms of musical competence, vocal control, and aural understanding further emphasizes the need for developing teaching procedures and activities which will take account of these differences and result in more effective learning on the part of all children. One is forced to question the continued acceptance of scheduling music classes and categorizing music activities in terms of grade level, per se.[8]

Contributions of Music to Child Development

It has been stated by many writers that children need—among other things—a sense of security, status in their group, opportunity for activity, and success in meeting some of their problems. Adults believe children also need to acquire worthwhile skills, to grow in understanding of their environment, and to develop attitudes in keeping with citizenship in a democracy. The music program can contribute to these needs in accordance with the quality of the music experiences, the organization of the program, and the teaching methods employed. Important contributions to the child's personal and social needs can be made, depending upon the manner in which music is taught, and upon the thoroughness and care with which the materials of instruction are organized.

A. A well-organized, consistent music program should:
  1. Result in sequential growth in music skills, habits, and attitudes;
  2. Provide for exploration in music related to children's activities at various developmental levels with a variety of materials. Attention should be concentrated on aspects of music that will afford breadth and depth of understanding.
B. The content of music can:
  1. Add to the understanding and enjoyment of life;

---

[8] Robert G. Petzold, "The Development of Auditory Perception of Musical Sounds by Children in the First Six Grades" (Madison, Wisconsin: School of Music, University of Wisconsin, n.d.), p. 32. Mimeographed.

2. Give understanding and appreciation of present-day living in the classroom, in the community, in the nation, and in the world;
3. Make more meaningful the history of our nation and of the world;
4. Present ideas reflecting worthy citizenship, good character, and spiritual development;
5. Add information or interest in other areas such as science, social studies, art, and health;
6. Suggest ideas for creative activities of many types;
7. Contribute to mental health through activities which are primarily recreational;
8. Give insight into the child's behavior and attitudes.

C. Good methods of teaching music should:
1. Cultivate individual interests and discriminating taste in a wide variety of music literature;
2. Stress pupil purposes and enjoyment as stimuli for developing musical interests;
3. Assist in developing group skills and habits through planning, sharing, and other group activities;
4. Help to discover thoughtful interpretation of musical performance, and critical thinking in the solution of musical problems;
5. Provide for maximum individual growth at individual rates and along different lines in order to produce those unique traits needed by creative artists and leaders in music;
6. Encourage experimentation and creativity on the child's maturity level.

Implications for Teaching Music

Some of the commonly accepted implications regarding the teaching of music which are based upon normal child growth and development follow:

Six-year-olds: Singing of little calls and phrases; stress on free rhythmic movement; rote singing; use of large size notation; listening often in terms of bodily response; individual and group experimenting with tones produced by a variety of basic media such as wood, metal, glass, and stone; brief music periods at several times throughout the day; providing for experience in choosing of songs, percussion instruments, and dramatizations; use of creative dramatizations, song improvisations, and expressive uses of percussion instruments; freedom for creativity under appropriate surveillance; song content about self, people, animals, and known things; both individual and group activity; tone-matching (listening) activities in appropriate songs, games, and dramatizations; many repetitions of simple tonal patterns.

Seven-year-olds: Extension of the general program for six-year-olds; rote singing; gradual recognition of note groupings; continued listening in terms of bodily movement; relation of bodily responses to simple note values; increasing use of metal keyboard instruments as well as the percussion instruments; individual and small group activity; tone-matching (listening) activities in appropriate songs, games, and dramatizations.

Eight-year-olds: Continuation and expansion of activities of seven-year-olds; songs of longer length; development of skill on keyboard instruments; rote and note singing; creation and reading of percussion scores; playing by some children on small blowing-type instruments; use of action songs; provision for individual differences; learning of new facts about notation; more critical and discriminating listening; dramatizations of music; more group activities; satisfaction of need to experience success; individual, small-group, and large-group activities; dialogue songs between boys and girls.

Nine-year-olds: Continuation of activities of eight-year-olds; instruction on band and orchestra instruments for those sufficiently mature; melody and keyboard instrument playing; use of notation; some rote singing; provision for individual differences with special individual and small-group work; music periods as long as thirty minutes; rounds, descants, simple part-singing; independent planning and working in music activities; creative experience in connection with all activities; dialogue songs; planning of experiences to develop confidence; relation of music content to concrete things; patriotic songs; more pupil participation in planning; folk-dancing; clear explanations of technicalities.

Ten- and Eleven-year-olds: Extension of the program for nine-year-olds; rhythmic activities to aid in bodily control and coordination; basic dance steps; provision for individual differences; planning of music activities to reduce antagonism between the sexes; importance of success in music; study of voice changes to come; band, orchestra, and chorus special groups; two- and three-part singing; increased teacher-pupil planning; continued creative work; more emphasis on music skills in activities purposeful to the children; sight singing; more analytical listening based upon aesthetic responses and consequent analysis.

Principles of Learning and Music

There are several principles that assist in the learning of music. These principles are based on how children grow, develop, and learn. They aid in the organization of music activities.

Learning is a process that changes an individual's behavior as he realizes purposes that are of value and meaning to him. Some conditions that help to bring about alterations in a child's behavior as he participates in music activities are as follows:

Readiness or maturation.   Children tend to learn best when what is taught is on their maturity level. Whatever is to be learned in music should be taught in relation to the physical, social, and intellectual capacity of the learner. His background of experience in music must be such that it will assist in the learning of needed skills, attitudes, appreciations, and understandings. Progressively more complex tasks should be planned by the teacher in such a way that frustration will be minimized and success more readily realized. Children should be physically, socially, and intellectually *ready* for a new learning experience.

A feeling of security and comfort.   Learning is facilitated when children feel secure and comfortable. Temperature, humidity, lighting, and appropriate periods of work and rest are among the items which make for physical security and well-being. The learner's ego needs and his self-concept should be such that they contribute to the learning process. One of the strengths of music in the curriculum is that it is a social art—something to be shared with others. An important objective of the teacher of music is that the individual be secure in his social environment—that he be respected and valued as a contributing member of the group and share in the pride of accomplishment of this group.

Provision for individual differences.   Children learn best when provision is made for individual differences. Because each child's background and rate of learning is different, identical learning situations will produce somewhat different results for different children. Teachers should find causes of poor responses, and modify learning activities accordingly. Superior responses of individual learners must be nourished, even though these good responses may cause the range of differences to become still greater. Music is particularly well-suited to provide for these differences because of the great variety of activities possible through which the different ability levels can be accommodated. Thus the teacher of music must know children's differences and music's versatility, and plan accordingly.

Motivation.   Children learn best when they are motivated. Means of motivating learning are always matters of prime consideration. Learning in music is motivated when children see meaning and purpose in what they are doing, when they are *active* participants either mentally or physically or both, and when they have a part in the planning so that the activity becomes theirs. *Variety* is also a natural means of motivation. Not only can music provide a variety of activities, but good planning will also provide variety—such as individual, small-group, and large-group participation—within a particular activity. Satisfaction and pleasure from experiences in music motivate learning. Success is an important motivating factor. Good teaching will make provision for these and for other types of motivation.

The environment.   Children tend to learn best in a rich and stimulating environment—in an environment rich in materials of instruction. Adequate numbers of music textbooks containing music of quality are necessary; at least one good basic music series in the classroom is essential with a second series available. Also necessary is musical equipment of quality, capable of establishing concepts of beauty in tone. Such equipment includes recordings, record players, tone bells, xylophones and pianos. Other items such as flannel boards or magnetic boards, and chalk liners, are also helpful. The most important environmental influence, however, is the teacher. Unless the teacher is musically sensitive, well-educated in music, and capable of transmitting his knowledge, his respect, and love for music to children, the materials mentioned above will not suffice. Furthermore, recent research in music has found the preschool musical environment in the home to be a highly significant influence in the learning of musical skills, attitudes, and appreciations in later years.

Problem-solving.   Children learn best when they understand the relationship between the musical activity and the purposes they are attempting to achieve. Music skills acquire true importance when they are needed to solve problems which are real to the learner. Interest in actively solving musical problems also becomes another motivating factor. In music activities are found superior examples of "learning by doing." The good teacher knows how to encourage children to "discover" a problem and to take part in planning how to solve it, helps them attempt to solve it and evaluate the extent of success achieved, and aids them in deciding whether the problem needs more attention and whether it has raised still other problems to be attacked later.

Practice is another aspect of problem-solving. Certain music skills require practice. If practice is to be of value as part of a learning process, the learner needs to know what this practice is to achieve in the solution of a musical problem. Therefore, he must understand the problem and its importance in the performance or understanding of music and he must feel the need of practice to try to solve the problem. He must practice something which relates clearly to the problem and constantly evaluate the effectiveness of the practice activity. Practice is more meaningful when the learner has a part in selecting the practice activities that he needs in order to realize his purposes or solve his problems.

Whole–part–whole.   Learning takes place best in situations where the learner understands the relation of the parts to the whole. For example, the learner understands an attempt to improve a part of a song if he has first heard the entire song and understands the relation of the part being studied to the entire song. This aspect of learning is simply another way of viewing the process whereby the learner understands thoroughly the purpose of what he is being guided to do. It is sometimes expressed as *synthesis-analysis-synthesis.*

Continuity.   Learning takes place best when there is continuity from activity to activity, from day to day, and from grade to grade. In the elementary school this requires that music be planned and taught in every grade in a manner that enables balanced musical growth to develop sequentially. Unless learning in any subject is presented with order and continuity, much of what has been learned is lost. Time spent by the good teacher and eager learner in one grade can be lost when continuity fails in the next grade. A balanced music program consists of a cluster of related activities, each of which needs continuity of development. The development of children's potential in music requires teachers who are competent in all these aspects.

Evaluation.   Learning is facilitated when an individual has a part in evaluating his performance. It is important to the learner (and therefore to the learning process) that he be provided with knowledge of his progress toward goals which he both understands and desires. There should be self-evaluation by both individual and group as an integral part of the learning process. It is best that the positive side of évaluation be emphasized first, with questions such as: "What did we do well today?" "In what ways did we improve?" "What did you like about what we did today?" Then, after these things are discussed: "In what ways can we improve?" "What might we do better tomorrow?" "How can we plan to take care of this?" This can constitute both evaluation and relation of one day's study to what will take place in tomorrow's music lesson.

Current Emphases in Music Education

The Maryland State Department of Education [9] lists some current emphases in music teaching that relate to the learning of both the children and teachers. They are as follows:

1. To keep music as a part of the self-contained classroom, with the classroom teacher playing an active role in providing and guiding the children's musical experiences.

2. To provide a flexible and consultative type of help for the classroom teacher through the leadership and partnership of the music specialist. (This emphasis is indicated through the newer job titles held by music specialists, such as "consultant" or "helping teacher.")

3. To use the characteristics of child development—physical, aesthetic, social, intellectual, and emotional—as key factors in determining the content and sequence of the music program.

4. To teach instrumental, vocal, and general music from the same philosophical and psychological bases.

5. To teach music through the use of music, rather than through talking about music. To illustrate: if a teacher finds it necessary, appropriate, or desirable to explain the meaning of a term such as *crescendo,* he will do so by singing or playing a musical composition in which the use of a crescendo is incorporated. Pupils will gain a working knowledge as well as a theoretical knowledge of the term through such teaching.

6. To regard music as a part of the total school curriculum rather than as an isolated area. Similarities to other areas are being used as bases for curriculum planning in order to make music a more

[9] *Music in Our Maryland Schools* (Baltimore: Maryland State Department of Education, 1959), pp. 7-8.

meaningful part of the curriculum. Differences are recognized, too, in terms of space, equipment, scheduling.

7. To teach music in a manner that will develop both skill and appreciation to the level that the pupil is capable of attaining.

8. To provide planned in-service training for classroom teachers and for music specialists.

To the above list can be added trends in the direction of the employment of more music specialists; the integration of certain aspects of vocal and instrumental music; the coordination of music activities in school and community; the increased emphasis on improving the quality of learning experiences in music and defining the purposes of music instruction; the inclusion of music as part of various school activities besides being a subject in its own right; the recognition of individual differences in children and the adoption of teaching methods to accommodate them; the provision of a greater variety of music books and other instructional materials; the teaching of music skills and notation in ways that emphasize interest, meaning, and use on the part of children; the development of a concept of music as a thinking, problem-solving activity; and the continuous evaluation of music programs with special emphasis upon children's use of music in their daily living.

CHAPTER IV

Evaluation of Music Achievement

Evaluation is an integral part of the process of music teaching. It reveals progress toward the objectives of the music program, provides evidence which should lead to the improvement of instruction, and provides motivation for both teacher and child. Measurement is only a part of evaluation. Measurement indicates how much has been learned, while evaluation is concerned with the quality of the whole process.

The clearly stated and well-understood objectives of the music program determine what should be evaluated. Since evaluation will attempt to determine the quality of the program, it is to be assumed that it should bring about improvements in it. Of course, the objectives should be carefully determined in relation to the capabilities of the children, and should be educationally defensible. The first three chapters have given some direction toward establishing objectives and curricula.

Measuring Children's Progress

Since music consists of many facets, arriving at a mark or grade which represents pupil progress is a complex matter. The chart on page 17 reveals this complexity. According to this chart, the teacher should be able to make a reasonably accurate estimate of the child's progress in listening-to-music skills, moving-to-music skills, and singing-and-playing skills. He should know to what extent progress has been made in developing enjoyment; creative capacities; knowledge of music literature; understanding of symbols, vocabulary, and structure of music; and in learning about humanity through music. Since a single grade should theoretically be dependent upon all these aspects of a good music program, it could be nothing but a generality. Therefore, it would seem that such a grade should be supplemented by written comments, or that more than one grade should be given.

Sources of evaluative information upon which grades may be

based include the information revealed to the teacher as the child takes part in various daily activities, informal tests (both tests of musical performance and written tests), standardized tests, and—in upper elementary grades—check lists of questions to assist the teacher and child in evaluating progress. The ability to determine a grade which purports to evaluate pupil progress rests upon a foundation of knowledge of the individual child. This means an awareness of his musical capacities, his maturity level, his home environment, his interests, and his social, emotional, and intellectual needs and maladjustments. The teacher should plan learning experiences based upon this knowledge, and then evaluate the child's musical growth and plan his musical needs.

The day-to-day observations of the teacher may be compiled through systematic use of anecdotal records. Progress charts, test scores, and cumulative report cards add information. The child should assist in determining his progress. The conference between the child and the teacher can be guided by a list of questions such as these:

> Has my ability to sing with pleasing tone quality, and with accurate pitch, improved? How has this been demonstrated?
> Do I play or sing alone before the class with more confidence? How do I show this?
> What have I learned about music reading and music vocabulary?
> What more can I hear now when I listen to music than I could last term?

An interesting study has been made comparing evaluation of children's performance in music with evaluation of their performance in other curricular areas. It is said that although a test score of 85 may be considered satisfactory in another subject, a child who sings or plays only 85 per cent of the notes of a song correctly would be considered to have made a poor showing in that particular musical response. The implication is that satisfactory musical performance requires perfect or near-perfect accuracy.

In teacher-made tests, it is best to devise questions based upon musical experience rather than upon the memorization of subject-matter facts about music. For example,

fact: Which instrument is a member of the woodwind family?
(a) clarinet, (b) trombone, (c) violin

musical experience: Name the instrument of the woodwind family
         which begins George Gershwin's *Rhapsody
         in Blue.*
fact: Write the key signature for the key of F Major.
musical experience: Why is B flatted in the key of F Major?

Short teacher-devised tests concerned with ear-training, such as those in which children write in notation the simple tonal combination the teacher plays or sings, are enjoyed by upper grade children and assist the learning of notation concepts. Other interesting short tests can be based upon listening to recordings.

Standardized tests are used infrequently in elementary schools. This often operates to the detriment of music in schools in which nearly all subjects are tested, for the teacher feels under pressure to emphasize the subjects in which progress is tested and tends to neglect subjects in which progress is not tested. One reason for the failure to test music progress is the variety of skills and knowledges which comprise a good music program—a variety which implies a battery of tests rather than a single test. Another is that music tests are said to be "notoriously unreliable and invalid." [1]

Standardized tests in music can be divided into three general classifications: tests of musical capacity, tests of musical interest, and tests of musical achievement.[2] Despite the above adverse comment, some tests—such as the Knuth Achievement Test,[3] designed for use in Grades 3–8 for testing understanding of notation—may be of real value.

Teacher-made tests and standardized tests should complement each other. Tests are valuable if interpreted correctly and if they result in curricular and instructional improvements and do not become ends in themselves.

Evaluating Music Programs and Music Teachers

Teachers and supervisors sometimes draw up a list of questions by which to evaluate the effectiveness of the music program or of

[1] Robert W. Lundin, *An Objective Psychology of Music* (New York: The Ronald Press, 1953), p. 227.

[2] Archie N. Jones, ed., *Music Education in Action* (Boston: Allyn and Bacon, Inc., 1960), pp. 346-49. The list of tests is helpful.

[3] Knuth Achievement Tests in Music (Minneapolis: Educational Test Bureau, Inc., n.d.). Recognition of rhythmic and melodic elements of music.

the teacher's work in music.[4] Thus the teacher can rate the program or himself, and the supervisor can do the same. Then the two meet to compare their ratings, discuss differences, and plan improvements. An entire school staff may rate the program in accordance with a list of questions relating to the objectives and the implementation of this program.[5]

Although music programs are seldom evaluated, most are in need of it. A certain informal evaluation is evident in the remarks teachers make in faculty rooms, but not enough formal evaluation takes place. In one school system, an evaluation stemmed from parents' protests to their board of education that their elementary school children were not receiving the education in music to which they were entitled. The board reacted by appointing a lay committee to evaluate the program. The committee responded by drawing up questionnaires to be answered by classroom teachers, principals and junior high school music teachers. The questionnaires were drawn up in such a manner as to permit the school staff to make its own evaluation. The result of this survey was that the elementary school music program was deemed in need of improvement, and the school district began experimenting with team teaching and with resource personnel to find remedies for the weaknesses revealed by the evaluation. Unfortunately such evaluations are the exception rather than the rule. Periodic evaluations by school authorities, and the improvements which result from them, are necessary if advances are to be made.

An administrator lists the following criteria concerning music offerings in the schools: They should be an experience of human value and a disciplinary experience; they should stir and intensify human emotions, satisfy a need for self-expression, recall solitude, interpret life, furnish worthy use of leisure time, furnish vocational skills, be a means of universal communication, furnish social pleasures, and develop a cultural heritage. He concludes his list with, "We must not leave the development of cultural taste to mere chance." [6]

[4] Frances M. Andrews and Clara E. Cockerille, *Your School Music Program* (Englewood Cliffs, N.J.: Prentice-Hall, Inc., 1958), pp. 263-68.

[5] *Music Education in Oregon Public Schools* (Salem, Oregon: The State Department of Education), pp. 99-100.

[6] William M. Lamers, "The Music Curriculum Present and Future," *Music Educators Journal* (April-May, 1961), 43.

Another writer presents still another criterion for evaluating the entire music program: "If music education is successful, it develops people who possess musical resources and musical competencies which enable them to make music a vital and moving force in their lives." [7]

To others, the success of an elementary music program may be measured by the proportion of the students who enter music classes in the secondary school. Another statement frequently heard is that the musical responsiveness of adults is the final criterion by which to judge the success of the school music program—a program necessarily based on the general music taught in the elementary schools.

Evaluative Criteria Checklist

The publication *Music in Our Maryland Schools* [8] includes a helpful checklist designed to assist school personnel and citizens of the community to answer the question, "How good is our school music program?" Following each statement are three columns headed "Yes," "No," and "Course of Action":

Classroom Activities

Activities are suited to the developmental level of the pupils for whom they are intended.

Activities are rooted in musical experiences.

Activities are so planned that they provide a "framework of action" for pupils.

Activities are so planned that there is an abundance of opportunities for pupils to learn through participation.

Activities are limited in scope to the extent that they enable pupils to achieve a satisfying mastery of materials and skills in a period of time suitable to their age group.

Activities can be evaluated in terms of enjoyment, understanding, and skill.

Activities are so planned that they lead logically from and into related activities and projects.

Activities are so planned that they provide for individual differences within the group.

Activities are based on what is known about human growth and development, and learning.

---

[7] Charles Leonard and Robert House, *Foundations and Principles of Music Education* (New York: McGraw-Hill Book Company, Inc., 1959), p. 16.

[8] *Music in Our Maryland Schools* (Baltimore: Maryland State Department of Education, 1959), pp. 215-18.

Activities take into account some of the important concerns of present-day living.

Activities give children opportunities to respond to music aesthetically, intellectually, and emotionally.

Activities help children foster the worth and dignity of each individual.

Activities develop the social relationships of pupils.

Pupil Growth

The pupil's attitude is becoming more favorable toward music.

Pupil discrimination and musical taste are improving.

The pupil uses music more wisely and more frequently both in and out of school.

The pupil sings and/or plays with more facility as a soloist and as a member of a musical group.

The pupil is developing an understanding of and an ability to use the components of music.

The pupil is developing a permanent singing, listening, and playing repertoire of musical value.

The pupil is developing an appreciation of detail and accuracy as a performer and consumer of music.

The pupil is developing his music talent to a maximum.

Teacher Growth

The teacher understands the purpose of music in the school program.

The teacher recognizes that music is an opportunity for pupils with varying interests and talents to grow intellectually, emotionally, and socially.

The teacher constantly evaluates his own musical values and interests.

The teacher knows and likes music.

The teacher is active in professional organizations.

The teacher participates in professional opportunities provided by the school.

The teacher works with other community agencies and institutions to improve the musical life of the community.

The School Music Program

Music is an accepted, integrated part of the school program.

The relationship between the elementary and secondary school music program is readily recognized.

The music program is a balanced program.

All students are given the opportunity to participate in music.

The music program is adequately financed.

The general and special music programs have equal status and opportunity.

Music staff loads are within reason.

Music teachers are well-qualified.

The music staff works cooperatively in setting up objectives and in achieving the objectives.

The music staff works cooperatively with other members of the school staff.

Secondary and elementary music teachers have opportunities to work together.

The principal provides orientation opportunities for new music teachers and in-service training opportunities for music staff members.

Physical facilities are designed and used in such a way that they provide for the growth and development of pupils.

Musical equipment is selected and used to meet the developmental needs of children.

All people concerned—teachers, principal, supervisor, parents, pupils—are continuously evaluating the music program in terms of its scope, sequence, and balance.

Pupils are aided through counseling in order to determine the extent of their participation in music activities.

CHAPTER V

Materials of Instruction

From the discussions in earlier chapters, certain guiding principles relating to the selection of materials of instruction can be formed. For example, since the recognition and understanding of beauty is a primary goal of music education, it follows that any sound-producing equipment—from a simple percussion instrument to a record player or piano—must be an instrument of quality which is capable of producing sound of aesthetic attractiveness which will assist the child in forming high standards of aural discrimination. Another obvious principle is that since musical backgrounds and capabilities of children result in a great many individual differences which must be accommodated, the materials of instruction of all types must be plentiful and varied. It is understood that the teacher of music must possess the knowledge of the subject and the understanding of children essential for the productive use of these materials. For example, a teacher with musical sensitivity and an understanding of how children learn will not use an untuned piano because only a properly tuned piano can produce beautiful sounds and because children learn to hear pitches and pitch differences accurately only when continually exposed to tones, intervals, and chords which are in proper tune.

Textbooks. The textbooks in music education are commonly called *music series books.* The writing, publishing, and selection of these books are quite commonly matters of controversy, *each from a somewhat different point of view.* The writers of these books are usually persons specially trained in the field; what they write is often influenced to a marked degree by publishers who must sell these books to remain in business. Since the buyers of the books influence the publishers quite decisively, it may be possible to credit the schools which use these books as the final arbiters of what goes into them. If these books are truly textbooks, there should be a good deal of musical learning set forth on their pages. If such material is in the books, this implies that the teachers are sufficiently well-educated in music to understand and to teach this material properly. Teachers' manuals, recordings, and piano accompaniment books are available with every standard series.

An examination of some of the series books published in the 1950's and earlier, indicates that there has been some deterioration in textbook quality; there seems also to have been a trend toward using these books primarily as song books for rote singing purposes. In 1956 Karl Gehrkens, early music series writer and one of the most experienced living music educators, declared that the quality of the song materials in the books was inferior to that in books published in the second and third decades of this century. He stated that later books were beautifully illustrated, but contained less attractive music.[1] When one publisher investigated the music series market several years ago, he found that although there was a good market for the books, there was a distressingly large number of classrooms in which the books remained unused on shelves because the classroom teachers were not able to teach the subject.

One set of series books is not sufficient to provide an adequate variety of source material. Therefore, a second series should be available if not actually in the classroom. Often a given classroom will have a book from one series for each child, and a second set of books of another series will be passed from room to room of that grade level as needed. However, some schools have as many as three complete sets of series books in each classroom from Grades 2-6.

Since music is a subject in its own right, music textbooks should be music-centered, and interrelationships with other curricular areas should be useful in enhancing the musical learnings which take place in the music class. However, outside the music period, music is very frequently employed to enhance other areas. Fortunately, music is so flexible a subject that good series books can be used for either purpose. However, selection of textbooks should be made primarily on the basis of the assistance such books give the teacher in helping children learn the subject, rather than for secondary considerations such as colorful art work or social studies content, important as these may be.

Recordings. The use of recordings to accompany series books is widespread, particularly in situations where the teaching staff

---

[1] Karl W. Gehrkens, "Five Decades of Music Education," *Education* (March 1956), 403.

lacks competency or adequate preparation in music. Such recordings can be useful in all situations when they provide appropriate specialized accompaniments to songs—accompaniments that would otherwise be impossible to provide. Classified lists of recordings recommended for school use can be found in catalogues of concern such as The Children's Music Center, 5373 West Pico Boulevard, Los Angeles 19, California, and The Teacher's Record Catalog, 274 Madison Avenue, New York 16, N.Y.

The teacher will find important assistance in his listening-to-recordings activities in record collections that include helpful suggestions for teaching, such as *Adventures in Music* RCA Victor Educational Records, 155 East 24th Street, New York 10, New York, the *Bowmar Orchestral Library* (including wall charts of the themes), Bowmar Educational Records, 10515 Burbank Boulevard, North Hollywood, California; and *Musical Sound Books,* a basic record library selected and annotated by the late Lillian Baldwin, available from the Sound Book Press Society, Inc., Scarsdale, New York, and also distributed by The Children's Music Center. Many school systems possess earlier sets of recordings such as the *RCA Victor Basic Record Library,* that include albums for listening, rhythm responses, and singing. These contain helpful teaching suggestions. There are many other specialized recordings and albums of recordings to be evaluated for classroom use. They can be found in the catalogues of the companies named above, and in catalogues of other concerns.

Recent music textbooks indicate that the trend toward the song book rather than the true textbook is being reversed, and that there is an increasing amount of music content in the textbooks.

In the 1950's *The American Singer Series,* published by the American Book Company, New York, N.Y., was a center of controversy. Its supporters lauded its note-reading plan while its detractors claimed that some of the contrived songs used to teach notational concepts were not sufficiently musical. No doubt there will be similar controversies in the 1960's.

Reading material.   There are books about music and composers written for children. These can be found listed in many college textbooks in this field, as well as in the catalog of The Children's Music Center. These belong in the school library for reference use and for special interest reading. Books written to be used by both children and teachers accompany the record collection selected by Lillian Baldwin. *Tiny Masterpieces for Very Young Listeners* (1958), published by Theodore Presser, Bryn Mawr, Pennsylvania, is written as a companion volume to the Baldwin recordings for the primary grades. *Music for Young Listeners: The Green Book, The Crimson Book, The Blue Book* (1951), published by Silver Burdett Company, New York, comprise a series written for use with the Baldwin selections for Grades 4, 5, and 6, respectively.

A popular periodical for children in Grades 4, 5, and 6 (to which they subscribe on a group basis) is *The Young Keyboard Junior,* (1346 Chapel Street, New Haven 11, Connecticut). This publication relates some of its content to radio and television performances of performing artists and conductors.

Pictures and charts. Music, like every other subject, has its illustrative materials. For example, teachers find and mount pictures of instruments and composers. Sets of such pictures can be purchased from commercial sources. Charts of note values, note patterns, and rhythm patterns are useful as visual aids in emphasizing various concepts of notation. Notation itself is a "picture" of what children have heard, and should be used consistently by teachers to explain "what it looks like when it sounds this way." The flannel board and magnetic board are useful because they eliminate the slow and sometimes faltering drawing of notation by the inexperienced, and because the notation made on them is good to look at. A music bulletin board has value, particularly when kept up-to-date. Some teachers include cartoons concerned with music to attract children to the bulletin board, where they are led to read other more serious things. Staff-liners and rolls of staff-lined butcher paper are convenient instructional aids. The keyboard, whether it be the piano, bells, xylophone, or a cardboard replica, is a visual aid of great significance in helping children understand notation. The Birchard Music Series includes supplementary charts to assist in teaching the understanding of music symbols and the playing of rhythm and tonal instruments.

16 mm films, filmstrips, and projectors. Films which are carefully previewed and selected, and which are presented to children with appropriate motivation and evaluation, assist learning. The very helpful *Film Guide for Music Educators* (1962), published by the Music Educators National Conference, 1202 Sixteenth Street

N.W., Washington 6, D.C., rates music education films under the headings: Musical Performance, History of Music, Band, Orchestra, The Teaching of Music, Visual Interpretation of Music, Acoustics, Music As a Career, and Music Festivals. A number of film strips are available. A good source is the Jam Handy Organization, 281 East Grand Boulevard, Detroit 11, Michigan.

Slide, opaque, and overhead projectors are useful teaching devices. Their advantages in teaching music parallel those in other areas.

Musical instruments. Keyboard, small wind,[2] and percussion[3] instruments have found increasing acceptance as part of the general music program equipment. The keyboard instruments include the piano, bells, and xylophone. Since they are audio-visual aids which help to explain the scale, intervals, and chords graphically, they have taken their place in the music-reading program and in adding interesting harmonic and aesthetic qualities to creative song interpretation and accompaniment. The purchaser should seek accurately-pitched instruments with superior tone quality.

The percussion instruments should also be evaluated on the basis of their attractiveness of sound. Only a minority of teacher- and child-made instruments will pass this test. Teachers should know the various instruments by name and type, and their uses in helping children learn basic rhythmic responses and patterns, dynamics, form, mood, notation, tempi, pitch, and creative interpretation.

Small wind instruments are produced by a number of manufacturers. The recorder-type and the flute-type are those most commonly used. Their functions include providing another type of playing experience and teaching notation in a practical situation. The major difficulty in their use is intonation.[4] The true recorder is regarded as the best of these instruments for use in the classroom.

Regular band and orchestra instruments are taught by instrumental music specialists. This opportunity begins ordinarily in Grades 4 or 5.

Other resources. Tape recorders can be a powerful stimulus in motivating improved listening and singing for both individuals and

---

[2] Robert E. Nye and Vernice Trousdale Nye, *Music in the Elementary School* (Englewood Cliffs, N.J.: Prentice-Hall, Inc., 1957), Chap. 3, "Teaching Melody and Harmony Instruments."
[3] *Ibid.*, p. 44.
[4] *Ibid.*, pp. 78-81.

groups. The record player is essential, of course. Both the tape recorder and the record player should be both sturdy and capable of high quality reproduction because superior tone quality is both a motivator and an essential part of teaching aesthetic appreciations. They should probably be purchased from companies which specialize in supplying schools with quality machines.

Radio and television are additional teacher aids. However, certain uses of them are controversial, as was brought out at the 1961 convention of the National Education Association,[5] when leading educators warned against misuse of these media which tended to place education in a lockstep and to destroy diversity. Unqualified acceptance of mass instruction via television was regarded as dangerous to good educational practices. These critics did not question the value of radio and television as teacher aids, but they did question their use in ways which made learning patterned and sterile, weakened the close relationship of student and teacher, and made the accommodation of individual differences unlikely. It is probable that competent teachers of music will seldom be interested in being part of a mass program for it, while those who are not competent will tend to use it as a substitute for not teaching it themselves, or as an aid in those areas in which they are deficient.

An item of equipment which appeared some years ago and is finding increasing acceptance is the record player with earphones. Like some teaching machines, it permits the child to be "alone," absorbed in his own problem-solving or enjoyment even though he is in a busy classroom. With his earphones he can "tune out" the activity around him. The music center is a table or area within a room which contains music, instruments, charts, pictures, and books which relate to the aspects of music being studied.

Field trips in which children visit musicians and musical events, and musician-citizens who come to the classroom to demonstrate, are part of community resources which should not be overlooked. Another source of assistance can be found in the resource guides prepared by state departments of education, county school systems, and city school systems. Some of these are of decided practical value. Teachers will find recent publications of this type reviewed or listed in various professional publications and periodicals.

5 "Explosion in the Schools: Quality Teaching," *Christian Science Monitor* (June 29, 1961).

CHAPTER VI

Plans of Organization

Descriptions of organizational plans are best understood in light of knowledge of the trend toward the self-contained classroom, which appears to have reached its zenith and is now in various stages of modification, and the decline of effective supervision of music in many of the schools in which the teaching of music is assigned to classroom teachers. The self-contained classroom situation is well-known, but the decline of supervision may need amplification.

Music supervision. Music was first introduced in the schools as a special subject taught by specialists. Later, for various reasons, the classroom teachers—who had been regarded as not competent to teach music—were assigned the task under the direction of music specialists whose responsibility was to see that those teachers, under close supervision and assistance, followed an imposed and inspected plan of teaching so that a sequentially-organized music program might exist in every grade throughout a school system. Such a plan was impressively successful in Minneapolis. Many large school systems adopted this supervisor-dominated plan, while many smaller systems tended to adopt the earlier type of organization in which the music specialist taught music in all the grades, and the classroom teachers had no specific responsibility for the subject. In both of these plans, however, the specialist was the authority for what was taught.

Into the twentieth century, the teacher education curriculum, which had begun with one year, was gradually lengthened to four. As the program was lengthened and improved, the professional stature of the classroom teacher began to grow. With this additional education, the teacher became generally more competent and was considered to be in less need of supervision. Also, since supervision is usually resented, there was a strong tendency in general education to reduce the authority of supervisors in all subject areas. Whereas the supervisor was once more powerful than the principal and the classroom teacher was virtually powerless, the relationship of these personnel changed. Today, the principal is often the supervisor of all subject areas, and the former supervisor has been reduced to a consultant's role. Since the principal is usually deeply involved in the myriad duties of his administrative office, he seldom has adequate time to supervise. There is also serious question that his professional preparation has given him sufficient knowledge in all subject matter areas to make him adequate for the task. Because the "supervisor" (actually a consultant) now often lacks specific authority, music supervision does not exist in some schools.

A characteristic of music education is that it has followed willy-nilly along whatever path education has chosen to travel at the moment. This fact of cooperation with general education should not necessarily be commended because, since music is essentially different from other subject areas, it cannot be assumed that whatever is best for education in general is therefore best for music. In this instance, we find classroom teachers with inadequate musical preparation working with the principal-supervisor who knows little more than they do about the subject, and the conscientious consultant reduced to a somewhat pathetic figure who goes about the schools hoping to stimulate interest in music teaching mainly by personal persuasion. In such school systems, an excellent music program may be described in printed materials designed to assist the room teacher, but the program actually followed in the schools may be quite another thing.

Supervision was originally instituted in American schools to insure that children had educational opportunities which teachers could not give them unless they received helpful and exacting supervision. Research shows clearly that the average classroom teacher of today is in need of expert supervision if the children are to receive the education in music to which they are entitled. Yet effective supervision is absent in many schools. It would seem that a return to some reasonable form of supervision is inevitable in view of the realities of the present situation in schools where the teaching of music is the responsibility of the room teacher.

Basic organizational plans. Educational theory places music in a highly strategic position. Besides being a subject in its own right, it helps to unify the curriculum and to illuminate the learning in other areas. It is evident that this cannot be fully accomplished by a music specialist. It is also necessary that the classroom teacher be involved in the music program and that he be sufficiently competent in music skills to utilize music at any time throughout the school day. This would be true even though a specialist taught music daily.

The minimum time allotment desirable for the elementary school music class is often stated as follows:

Kindergarten	30 minutes daily (interspersed throughout the day)
Primary Grades	20 minutes daily (and for additional brief periods incidentally)
Upper Grades	25 minutes daily

Although the number of organizational plans is myriad, they tend to cluster about five major types in which the principal is often the overall supervisor. Under these plans:

1. The classroom teacher is responsible for music instruction.

2. The classroom teacher is responsible for music instruction with assistance from a consultant, who may be on call.

3. The classroom teacher is responsible for music instruction in the primary grades with consultant assistance; the music specialist on schedule is responsible for music instruction in the intermediate grades.

4. The music specialist does scheduled teaching in each classroom each week, and the classroom teacher is responsible for music instruction on the days the specialist is not available.

5. The music specialist has full responsibility for a departmentalized music program.

It is difficult to determine which of these plans is the one most commonly employed. Preston states:

> In practice, most schools deviate somewhat from the strict self-contained pattern by providing partial departmentalization in the intermediate grades. This affords needed relief to the regular teacher and gives the children direct contact with more than one teacher —usually a wholesome and stimulating experience.[1]

He adds that most of the departmentalization is in music, art, and physical education. Many studies point out that the strictly self-contained classroom plan is the least desirable in practice for music.[2] In recent years a number of comments which resemble statements

---

[1] Ralph C. Preston, *Social Studies in the Elementary School* (New York: Holt, Rinehart & Winston, Inc., 1958), p. 6.

[2] A. Verne Wilson, "The State of Music Education," *Music Educators Journal* (September-October, 1956), 30.

of thirty and forty years ago have become increasingly common. For example:

> The ideal situation is a combination of the self-contained classroom and the platoon system classroom. . . . Under this plan, the classroom teacher would be responsible for all subjects except art, music, and physical education. Thus the children would be taught music by a qualified specialist in a room that is equipped only for that purpose.[3]

It should be noted that the one plan which has continued serenely through these controversial days is the strict music specialist plan in which the specialist is fully responsible for music (the classroom teacher rests or performs other school duties while the specialist teaches her group). This does not conform to current educational theory, but the plan has operated to the satisfaction of those schools which retained it. Wilbur J. Peterson's study [4] of these various plans reveals that administrators who employ the specialist plan prefer it to all others; that administrators who employ the plan in which classroom teachers are responsible for music with little or no assistance from specialists desire that visiting specialists on schedule be added; and that administrators who permit teachers to "trade" music in exchange for some other subject desire a change to a scheduled specialist plan which also involves classroom teacher responsibility in primary grades, and to this same plan for intermediate grades *or* to complete departmentalization in Grades 4, 5, and 6.

A study that compares the results of these plans is Hermann's,[5] which is limited to sight-reading achievement. In each type of test employed in the study, the completely self-contained classroom with consultant service and with supervision by the principal rated lowest in achievement. The one plan which was rated slightly superior to the music specialist plan was one in which music was taught in Grades 1–3 by classroom teachers for whom music teaching competency was a condition of employment and whose teaching included

[3] Roger B. Phelps, "Music in the Self-Contained Classroom," *Music Educators Journal* (February-March, 1957), pp. 36-38.

[4] Wilbur J. Peterson, "Organization Plans Favored by Administrators for Elementary School General Music," *Music Educators Journal* (January, 1957), 48-51.

[5] Evelyn Hermann, "A Comparison Study of the Sight-Reading Ability of Students Taught by the Music Specialist and of Students Taught by the General Teacher in a Self-Contained Classroom" (Doctoral dissertation presented at the University of Oregon, 1962), p. 66.

regular visitation-type supervision by a music specialist, and in Grades 4–6 by music specialists.

Currently there are a number of experiments taking place in self-contained classroom schools. These include team teaching and teaching by "resource" personnel. They constitute steps toward specialization in that the person most competent to teach the subject does so.

Instrumental music. Instrumental music has remained in the hands of music specialists through the years. School systems commonly provide opportunities for children to begin instruction on band and orchestra instruments in the intermediate grades. At this age the child is intellectually active and enjoys investigating new avenues of expression. He also has the ability to concentrate for longer periods of time, and he possesses a more critical attitude toward his musical performance. However, he needs reasonable drill and repetition in order to achieve his goals as an instrumentalist. Because the child forms basic social attitudes at this age, and because he needs to feel secure in his social group, it is logical for him now to learn to work in an instrumental group and to develop group loyalty. The degree of exactness necessary for an instrumental (or choral) group to function helps to develop basic respect for high standards of accuracy.

Instrumental music classes are often organized semi-independently of the basic general music program. However, the specialized instrumental program should be an *outgrowth* of a good general music program, not something unrelated to it. A common complaint of instrumental music teachers is that children learn little in general music classes that will function in or apply to their work in instrumental music. Perhaps the most frequent complaint is that the child comes to them "not knowing one note from another." Although the general music program exists for different purposes and its primary function is not as a "pre-band" or "band-recruitment" curriculum, the instrumental and general music program should be sufficiently coordinated so that the instrumental teacher will be unable to continue his complaint that the intermediate-grade children come to him with no understanding of music notation or music vocabulary. There should be joint planning between the instrumental teacher and general music teacher in an organizational plan in which each teacher understands his part in the overall music program.

A common complaint of classroom teachers is that the plan under which the instrumental music teacher must work often necessitates the interruption of the school day for those students who take part in band and orchestra classes. Although there is no known way fully to overcome this objection, it may help the situation psychologically if the classroom teachers, the music teacher, and the principal plan together to schedule the instrumental classes in a way that works the least possible hardship on the classroom teacher. This is in contrast to an all too common situation in which the schedule is handed to the classroom teacher by edict from the principal's office.

CHAPTER VII

The Preparation of the Teacher of Music

To introduce this subject and the spirited controversy which rages around it, let it be said that there should be no quarrel over *who* will teach music. There should, however, be concern over the competency of anyone assigned to this work. One might begin from the position that only a person who thoroughly understands both music and children should teach the subject. The reader should keep in mind that a shortage of both classroom teachers and elementary music specialists casts a complicating shadow over the entire problem. Another factor in elementary education, which is often exasperating to those who understand the area, is the tendency of many educators in secondary schools and colleges to equate "elementary" with "simple." There is no more complex field in education than elementary education, and teaching general music in grade school is indeed more complex than teaching high school chorus. Many a choral specialist has found failure and frustration when attempting to teach music in a first grade classroom where half of the children may not yet be able to match tones. To teach music in the primary grades demands first-rate musicianship and first-rate understanding of the individual child and his musical problems.

The Classroom Teacher

In the 1930's, educational theory which led to the concept of the completely self-contained classroom combined with the financial crisis of that decade to promote a type of school organization in which the influence of the music specialist tended to be reduced or entirely eliminated, and the classroom teacher was given increasing responsibilities for music teaching. The reverberations of this change have not ceased.

Rose Phillips, speaking before a gathering of elementary school principals in 1924, said that most classroom teachers were not specially trained in music, yet they were expected to produce excellent results in teaching it. Then she praised the platoon school, a type of departmentalized school, because the classroom teacher in such a school was relieved of this burden and a specialist trained in music was assigned to teach it.[1] In the same year, speaking at the Music Supervisors National Conference, Edward B. Birge said:

> I am not finding fault with the grade teacher. She does her best to carry out her part of a contract which asks too much of her. . . . We ought to look ahead and plan for the day when music will not be taught by grade teachers but by specialists who are inspired and inspiring teachers, musicians by instinct and cultivation. . . . There are signs on the educational horizon which encourage the belief that we are beginning to move in this direction. The platoon school, for example, is rapidly making a place for itself.[2]

Birge's comment is of interest today, when the content of his remarks are being stated again. In the version of the 1960's, it is expressed as favoring a modified self-contained classroom which permits specialists to teach music.

To gain further perspective in attempting to solve today's problems, we should examine situations in which the classroom teacher is successful in teaching music. An example is found in the elementary schools of Austria and Switzerland—countries that have no shortage of teachers. There, elementary school children receive 100 minutes of music instruction per week by classroom teachers, all of whom are considered competent to teach the subject. This time allotment continues through each year of high school until the final two years, when the student may choose between music and art. The teacher education program is one of five years' duration. The prospective teacher receives an average of 100 minutes of music instruction per week in each of the five years. Thus, these classroom teachers have many years of consistent education in music. Should the prospective teacher reveal ineptitude in music, he is barred from entering the teaching profession. After he begins to teach, should a state inspector find that he cannot teach music satisfactorily, he can be relieved of his certification. It is easily understandable why the classroom teachers in these countries are qualified to teach music to children.

---

[1] Rose Phillips, "Platoon Schools of Detroit," *Third Yearbook* (Elementary School Principals, National Education Association, 1924), p. 535.

[2] Edward B. Birge, "The Future of America Rests with the Schools," *Journal of Proceedings,* Music Supervisors National Conference, 19 (1926), 177.

In some elementary schools in the United States, classroom teachers are excellent teachers of music. This is made a condition of employment, and if it is found that a teacher cannot teach music satisfactorily, he is replaced by one who can. Such situations, not uncommon years ago, appear quite harsh to present-day teachers whose experience in the profession has been limited to the years of teacher shortage. It does not appear strange to those who remember the days of teacher surplus, nor does it appear strange to taxpayers who expect high standards of performance of the teachers they employ.

The elementary teacher education curricula in the United States require very little preparation in music. In fact, the proportion of the curriculum devoted to music has declined as the number of years of preparation has increased.[3] Some states require only one quarter or one semester of college work in music, and even this is in some places interpreted as comprising any music course—even one which has no direct application to teaching in the classroom. A course sequence of one academic year's duration is found to be somewhat above-average. Since many college students today have had little or no music training in the elementary schools, and perhaps none at all in the secondary school, it becomes apparent that many of the students destined to teach music will have had little or no experience with the subject before this brief contact with it in college. There is a convincing amount of research which shows that the average classroom teacher of music accomplishes little more than some rote singing and the occasional use of a phonograph record, and that the supervising staff in many schools ignore the situation because they cannot remedy it under present conditions.

The plight of the unmusical or inadequately educated teacher compelled to teach music has attracted wide sympathy. For publishers, it has been something of a bonanza, for they have sold in large volume many publications which state with great optimism that anyone can teach music. For example, one company went so far as to claim that even a teacher "who couldn't carry a tune in a bucket" could, with the aid of its publication, "give her class vivid experiences in music."

---

[3] Abraham A. Schwadron, "The Music Preparation of the Classroom Teacher" (unpublished paper presented at the School of Fine and Applied Arts, Boston University, 1960).

To remedy this embarrassing situation, in-service training has been advanced as a solution. One study revealed that initial progress can be made by this means. The researcher concluded that a primary cause of musical inadequacies of classroom teachers was insufficient or ineffective music education during childhood, and that most college courses as currently organized fail to overcome this insufficient or ineffective music education. He recommended that "since most musical skills and knowledges require extended periods of time to be mastered, college departments of education should consider plans to extend their present music courses for elementary classroom teachers over a two or three year period even though this may necessitate proportionate reduction in the number of hours allotted to music per year." [4]

Two studies arrived at identical conclusions: that it requires a minimum of three academic years of college music training to prepare the average classroom teacher to become competent in teaching music. One of these is the Barbour study.[5] The second one, the Belstrom study,[6] found the majority of workers in the field "more than moderately dissatisfied" with the greater part of the training in music. According to this study, no teacher training institution in the United States was found to have an outstanding program which produced elementary education graduates well-prepared to teach classroom music. Belstrom pointed out the three areas of necessary preparation as music theory, methods, and appreciation.

As early as 1947, the Music Education Curriculum Committee of the Music Educators National Conference stated: "It is believed that *not less* than eight semester hours should be allowed by the teacher training institution to attain the desired goals." [7] Today, fifteen years later, it is evident that this statement was an under-

---

[4] Robert B. Glasgow, "A Study and Evaluation of an In-Service Training Class in Music for Elementary Teachers" (Doctoral dissertation presented at the University of Oregon, 1961), pp. 81-82.

[5] Richard Elliot Barbour, "A Survey and Evaluation of the Music Courses Offered in Maine Training Schools for Prospective Classroom Teachers" (Master of Music Education thesis presented at the University of Boston, 1953), pp. 52-54.

[6] LaVere E. Belstrom, "A Study of the Pre-Service Training of the Elementary Teacher in the Teaching of Music" (Doctoral dissertation presented at the University of Colorado, 1950), p. 382.

[7] Music Education Curriculum Committee, *Music Education Source Book* (Chicago: Music Educators National Conference, 1947), p. 38.

estimate of the time needed at the college level to render most of today's elementary education majors competent to teach music.

College courses in music education for the classroom teacher have made progress in recent years. In an earlier day, the content of music fundamentals (simple theory) classes often consisted of the facts of music theory; today the content is predominantly experiences in music which relate directly to teaching it in the classroom. Much of this work is of precollege level, and a question could be raised as to whether or not college credit should be granted for elementary-school level content.

One commonly found weakness in college music work is the inadequacy of the student teaching program. Not infrequently the student teacher must be placed in the classroom of a public school teacher who teaches little or no music under the supervision of a general education supervisor from the college who is equally lacking in music competency. In these situations, everyone is apt to ignore music, and the student teacher may wonder why the music courses were in the college curriculum in the first place.

To strengthen music education in the elementary schools in which the classroom teacher is responsible for music, changes must and will be made. Ideally, the prospective teacher should have been exposed to a good music program from kindergarten through high school. The college should organize a music program that provides opportunity for the student progressively to develop music skills and knowledges over an extended period of time and presents a student teaching situation that provides significant experiences in music teaching under the guidance of musically competent supervisors. After this, the schools should employ only those teachers capable of teaching music to children. Finally, the school music program should be adequately supervised.

The Music Specialist

The Committee Report on Graduate Study in Music Education states:

> The development of the music teacher is more complicated and more involved than the preparation of the teacher of academic subjects. The teaching of music in the schools employs so many facets of training that it is almost universally recognized among musicians

that the four year baccalaureate degree program is inadequate to develop a desirable degree of musical competence.[8]

When the music major enters college, his aim is nearly always to be the director of a high school band, orchestra, or chorus. This is a natural result of his very recent success and pleasure in participating in high school music groups. It is ordinarily not until his junior-year music methods courses that he realizes that to be a music educator means that his interest in teaching music must include the elementary grades and the junior high school as well. He then learns that music is a twelve- or thirteen-year program which involves far more than the senior high school. He comes to understand that music is an area, not a subject, and that music education is a cluster of specialties: band, orchestra, chorus, elementary general music, and junior high school general music. He begins to understand that although music history, literature, and theory are possible class offerings in high school, they also are threads which tie the various aspects of the twelve-year program into an integrated, coordinated whole. Then, with student teaching in both elementary and secondary school, he consciously *adds* elementary music education to his secondary school specialty. Thus, the number of music majors who initially elect elementary music as a primary teaching area is few. The specialist is more likely to gravitate toward specializing in elementary school music rather than to plan on doing this in the first place. The shortage of specialists in this area has been aggravated by the emphasis in the literature of the 1950's on the teaching of elementary music by the classroom teacher.

The program of studies of the music major is arduous, and is often little understood by the nonmusician. Unlike majors in other areas, he knows his goal when he enters college and begins his freshman year with applied music, ensembles, theory, and perhaps music literature as a liberal arts elective. Music majors are professionally-minded, and unite—thousands strong—in the student chapters of the Music Educators National Conference. When the music major becomes a teacher, he joins with tens of thousands of other school music teachers to make the Conference the largest subject matter department of the National Education Association.

[8] Committee Report, "Graduate Study in Music Education," *Journal of Research in Music Education* (Fall, 1954), 160-61.

The music educator commonly sees no basic difference in the musical preparation of the elementary music specialist and the secondary music specialist. There is general belief that to be a musician requires the same basic preparation in theory, sight-reading, ear-training, and music literature, and the same level of performance ability. It is recognized that there is insufficient time in the curriculum to gain some other knowledges that are valuable in teacher education. One elementary specialist writes:

> An elementary music teacher who is expected to teach a different group every twenty minutes must have a thorough knowledge of group dynamics and psychological implications of behavior patterns, and an extreme sensitivity to individual problems and ability levels in the classroom to teach effectively. Unfortunately, background in music education does not always include such training.[9]

In most curricula, a course in human growth and learning is required of all education majors. However, there is often dissatisfaction with these courses because the education generalist who normally teaches them is seldom able to relate their content specifically to music teaching.[10]

There exists a belief in some circles that education in music should be confined to a maximum of two years in a four-year degree program. Music educators advance two major reasons to the contrary: (1) because music is a performing art, it is imperative that music students be actively learning and improving in a number of aspects of musical performance during their entire degree program, and (2) it is necessary to educate the music major in basic musicianship during the first two years of a four-year program in order that he may achieve sufficient competence as a musician to be able to succeed in the courses required in the last two years. The first statement is generally understood and needs no amplification. For example, the following recommendation was supported unanimously at the 1961 meeting of the Higher Education Section of the Eastern Division of the Music Educators National Conference:

---

[9] Dorothy Lobbato, "The Eternal Triangle," *Oregon Music Educator* (March-April, 1960), 17.

[10] Frank Woost, "A Survey of Opinions Concerning the Adequacy of Preparation for Music Teaching by Graduates of the Schools and Colleges of California" (master's thesis presented at the San Diego State College, 1961).

That recognition be made of the fact that the distinguishing feature of the music teacher is his ability to communicate with his students via musical skills and in terms of musical concepts, and that his knowledge of musical subject matter is primarily gained through musical performance. Such skills and concepts must be developed without interruption over a long period of time. To defer them until the final years of college or until graduate study is to produce an ineffective teacher who must rely almost exclusively upon verbalization skills for the teaching of a nonverbal art.

The second statement is less well understood. The two-year theory (harmony) course is basic to the education of all music majors. It concerns certain elements of music science—largely how music is constructed from a chordal viewpoint. Students learn of chord construction and about chord progressions. They learn fundamental laws of harmony and they learn to hear, identify, and analyze chords and chord tones by listening to them and by writing them. They learn of triads, seventh and ninth chords, altered chords, chordal modulations, nonharmonic tones, and harmonic rhythm. Combined with this in most theory courses are sight-reading, ear-training, keyboard harmony, and some creative composition relating to the study of harmonic analysis. Only after the music student has learned to hear and analyze the structure of music can he conduct a choral or instrumental group with musical understanding. A conductor must instantly hear and analyze all that is being sounded in a choral or instrumental rehearsal or in an elementary school singing lesson. The successful study of harmony makes this possible. Sight-reading assists melody analysis and ear-training assists in analyzing both chords and melodies. The person who conducts music classes without this understanding of music structure is a mere "time beater," not a musician. Therefore, the idea that a music education degree can somehow be compressed into a two-year program of music studies is not taken seriously by music educators. The basic theory course operates as a screening device; the student of below-average ability in theory is usually advised to change his field.

After the basic theory courses, the student is assumed to be ready for required courses in conducting, arranging, music methods, form and analysis, and eventually student teaching. He also becomes eligible for electives such as advanced courses in counterpoint and composition although these are sometimes required. Although there have been statements made—with some logic—to the effect that a teacher of elementary school music may not need as much musical training as a secondary school music teacher, such statements have met with little response. Nearly all music education majors are secondary education majors who *add* elementary music education courses to their curriculum. Also, it seems just as necessary to have musicians in elementary schools as it is to have them in secondary schools. Furthermore, music teachers wish to be qualified to teach at all levels, and do not elect degree programs that would confine them to the elementary school.

The undergraduate preparation of the music major is subject to unusual difficulties because of the demands of the public schools that most graduates be able to teach a number of different specialties within the music area. The attempt to prepare these majors properly for such eventualities severely limits the time they have to do much else. The fact that in most high schools the students are restricted to only one musical activity, either vocal or instrumental, compounds the problem in the colleges. The same schools that have these restrictions which produce an unbalanced musical development in students will frequently expect the young college graduate to be fully prepared to teach all of the different musical specializations. Education needs some plan whereby the future music teacher is identified in the public schools and is given a balanced and varied musical diet there before entering college. A recent study recommends that: "Training to teach music at both elementary and secondary levels is necessary for all teachers since so many teaching assignments in music require this combination," and states that the same thing is true concerning a combination of instrumental, vocal, and general music.[11] The study also states that there should be no reduction in methods courses and student teaching, adding that there was some evidence that these requirements should be increased. Consequently, the typical curriculum emphasizes musical and professional courses, and this tends to limit the amount of general education attainable. Thus, a major issue concerning music education curricula is the amount of general education possible in a program of studies which properly equips the student to teach his subject in the schools. There is little agreement found when the issue is examined on a world basis. For example, a teachers college at

---

[11] *Ibid.*

Adelaide, Australia, has a curriculum consisting of 27 units. The division of these units for the music education major is as follows: professional education, 3 units; general education, 3 units; music, 21 units. From the viewpoint of one professor at this college, the program of music courses required of the major in many American colleges is quite inadequate to prepare school music teachers.

A standard curriculum for the American music educator is that established by Dr. Karl Gehrkens at Oberlin College. In this historic curriculum, music was allotted half of the four-year program of credit hours, and professional education and general education were each allotted one quarter. Though the Gehrkens curriculum is one approved by most music educators, recent years have seen a decline in the amount of music in many curricula owing to the pressure of other areas, particular general education. A recent example of this has come from the National Council for the Accreditation of Teacher Education (NCATE), an organization that is attempting to exercise, through accreditation, some degree of control over all teacher education in the United States. Its influence is currently being used in some institutions to reduce the hours of specialization and professional education, and to increase the amount of general education in all areas of teacher training. Since the professional music educator believes that a somewhat opposite course is essential in order to prepare qualified music teachers, a new crisis is forming at the college level. If the present inclination of this accrediting association prevails, there is a strong possibility that music education will suffer both in teacher quality and teacher supply. The reaction of many college music faculties is exemplified in the following resolution passed unanimously by a music faculty and presented to a state department of education: "The preparation of the teacher of music is such that it cannot be equated with that of other areas; this should be recognized in any attempt to standardize teacher education." [12]

Paralleling the influence of NCATE have been similar efforts by some state departments of education to expand the amount of general education uniformly in all teaching fields, regardless of their basic differences. Allen P. Britton writes that some recent state certification laws have raised general education requirements in excess

---

[12] Resolution of the faculty of the School of Music, University of Oregon, February 1, 1962.

of NCATE recommendations, and adds: "Whether music teachers can be properly trained under the provisions of these laws is a serious question." [13]

It is of interest in view of these trends to reduce the amount of music which a music major may have in his degree program to note that the most frequent criticism of these majors voiced by school administrators who employ them is: "The graduates are too specialized; they need to be educated more generally *in music*." This practical criticism from the field should be heard by the colleges and by those with little familiarity with the field who would reduce the music preparation of the music major.

This criticism means that the administrators want music teachers prepared to teach two or more of the various specialities that comprise the area of music education; it also implies the need for additional preparation in music.

However, it is possible that some administrators may not accept the conclusion implied by this statement, and that they may believe that a radical change is necessary in order to alter the music education curriculum in a way that will permit a larger portion of the student's time to be spent in nonmusic courses.

There is some disagreement among music educators concerning whether or not they themselves might have made curricular errors in recent decades. For example, a director of music in a large city system tested all applicants for music positions by asking them to sing at sight songs of average difficulty from 6th- or 7th-grade music series books. He found that half these music graduates were "completely unable" to do this. He further found that some of them could not identify the fact that some melodies were written in the minor mode. It was his claim that the musicians themselves have, over the years, added courses in instrumental techniques at the expense of needed courses in sight-reading, basic musicianship, and music history and literature. However, it would seem that to correct such a situation would require a larger proportion of music courses than ever.

In attempting to solve many educational problems, it is commonplace for the colleges to place some responsibility at the door of the secondary school. Although the tendency to blame the educational

---

[13] Allen P. Britton, "Music Education in the Nineteen-Sixties," *Music Educators Journal* (June-July, 1961), 26.

level from which students come for omissions in their education is an overworked concept, it seems true that until there are music content courses in the high schools, the colleges and universities have a disproportionate burden when they must begin the education of most music majors at what is in fact a very low precollege level. This is one reason why the music major of today must have the larger part of his collegiate education made up of music courses—a proportion that often shocks educators in other fields. If American high schools had the type of program that is found in several European countries, it is possible that the first year of theory, the introductory music literature course, and courses in beginning piano could be eliminated from the college curriculum, and the time saved could be added to other courses. Currently, there are efforts being made to offer special first-year theory and music literature courses by colleges to high school students who plan to become music majors. Although such moves have serious geographical limitations in that only students in the immediate area of the college would usually have access to the courses, they constitute a step toward the time when current college music courses required in the freshman year may be completed before the music major enters the college. Private piano teachers offer potential assistance in that some may be able to teach their students a sufficient amount of theory to enable them to begin their college work with the second year of theory by passing an examination in the content of first-year theory.

One logical answer to the problem of the crowded music education curriculum which finds almost universal support is that it be made a five-year curriculum. The major objection to this lies not in such a curriculum, but in the comparison of it with those of other teacher preparation fields. There is a strong trend toward the five-year program in general education whereby the student can obtain the baccalaureate degree at the end of four years, and the master's degree at the end of the fifth year. Because of the situation peculiar to music, the five-year program in music education appears likely to be necessary to obtain the baccalaureate degree. Such a situation would place the music education major under a handicap and would in turn tend to reduce teacher supply in music.

In summary, it is difficult to prepare qualified elementary music specialists for a number of reasons, one being that they are normally majors in the secondary school area with preparation in the elementary area an added segment of their basic curriculum. The attempts of various educational bodies to impose uniform standards in teacher preparation, particularly in the amount of general education required, threaten to reduce further the quality and supply of elementary music specialists.

CHAPTER VIII

Selected Issues and Related Research

Research in music education. Much research on music education has been completed in recent years. This is largely the work of graduate students in colleges and universities. In advanced-degree research, equal emphasis is often placed upon (1) the content of the study, and (2) the demonstrated use of various research techniques by the candidate. The research subject must no longer be entirely original; there are too many researchers now at work to insist upon this.

The mass of information concerning music education is not accumulated in one place, nor is it evaluated and organized so that unquestioned conclusions can be made from assembled evidence. To do this would require the time of persons who know this area very well, and the money to sustain them while they labored with this important task. Therefore, any writer who quotes from this research does so knowing only a fragment of it, and the reader should understand and interpret his work accordingly. However, it is true that much of what is of value comes to light in educational publications, so that if a writer keeps in touch with what is being written and reported, his views are likely to reflect general situations with fair accuracy.

It is wise to judge each research effort as a "straw in the wind" rather than as conclusive evidence. When these "straws" cluster together and point in the same direction, then the evidence may be assumed to be conclusive.

The opinions of respondents to questionnaires form an important part of many studies in education. Although the questionnaire is not a very accurate technique of research, it is sometimes the only one which is practical. After the researcher obtains his questionnaire findings, he must properly interpret them. If he lacks the background to interpret his findings, or if the area of his study is too broad to include sufficient specific findings, his research may be of little value.

One of the more difficult types of research to conduct is the broad curriculum study which attempts to include all the areas of instruction in elementary education. In these, opinions related to music are sought along with opinions related to all the other subject areas.

Some of these studies seek opinions concerning items such as the value of a college course (great? average? little? none?) to the respondent. Any reply the respondent gives is an opinion based on many different factors. Unless this opinion is analyzed to find the reason why the respondent made the particular response he did, it may have little meaning. For example, the author has examined studies of this type which endeavor to reveal the value of college music education courses, and has found that entirely different conclusions are drawn by different researchers from essentially the same evidence. When some studies reveal that respondents rate the music methods course low in relation to other courses, researchers have variously found or concluded that (1) the music methods course is so well-taught that it can be reduced in required hours, (2) the course is of no value to the respondent, because the administration does not require that the respondent try to teach it, (3) a specialist teaches music and the respondent has no time for it in her daily schedule, (4) the music offerings of the college must be greatly strengthened and credit hours must be added to insure that teachers in the future will find more value and use for music in the curriculum, and (5) the college methods class is so badly taught that it has little value.

Such confusion shows that this type of broad curriculum study might well be limited to smaller areas of deeper penetration. Attention is drawn to it here to suggest that the reader analyze such studies with care before accepting their conclusions as valid.

The phrasing of questions is extremely important. "Which do you prefer?" and "Which is best for the education of children?" are two very different questions that are sometimes erroneously equated. A teacher might answer the first question in terms of what is more convenient for himself, while the second question demands consideration of what is best in the education of children. Thus, the same group of teachers may respond quite differently to these questions. There are, of course, many research procedures, of which the questionnaire is only one.

A massive compilation and classified organization of research titles in music education is currently being undertaken under the auspices of the Music Education Research Council, directed by Dr. Roderick Gordon, of Boston University. Since it will be the first complete listing of such titles, it is expected to be of great assistance to future researchers.

The selected issues which follow have already been mentioned and discussed in some degree in preceding chapters, and have been the subjects of research which has also been reported earlier. Here they will be further defined and discussed.

The classroom teacher as music teacher versus the music specialist as music teacher.   The belief that the classroom teacher should teach music has been very persistent, and there is convincing educational theory to support it. The concept of the self-contained classroom as the best way to organize elementary education became gradually dominant from the 1930's up to the present. Recently, the concept has been subject to a number of modifications, and there is some retreat from the position that the more self-contained the educational plan, the better it is. The true issue, which is often obscured, resolves itself around music teaching competency. It does not matter who teaches music; what is important is that the child receive the instruction in music to which he is entitled and for which the taxpayer is presumably paying.

Theoretically, there seems little question that the classroom teacher is the person best situated to teach music. He is with the children all day and thus can utilize music for various purposes outside the music lesson. It is asserted that he understands the children better than a visiting specialist, and thus should be able to accommodate individual differences in music more skillfully. Because he teaches the entire curriculum, he should be in a superior position to relate music to the other areas of instruction when it is desirable to do so.

When the trend toward the self-contained classroom became evident, some music specialists believed that if this plan of organization seemed good for teaching other subject areas, it should therefore be good for teaching music. The immediate task seemed to be to convince the classroom teacher that this was so, and the textbook writers did their best to oblige: "Every classroom teacher can teach music successfully"; [1] "In order to teach music successfully, the classroom teacher does not have to know the techniques of music, as helpful as these might be. What he does need is a certain attitude and spirit"; [2] "If you have the right point of view, the right approach in bringing music to your children, then many seeming impossibilities are at once and amazingly transformed into possibilities." [3] Later, Marguerite Hood commented on music in the self-contained classroom:

> In schools where there is enough assistance for the classroom teacher by special music teachers to insure for the children a good, continuous, and well-balanced music curriculum, this idea works. But when unskilled classroom teachers are thrown almost entirely on their own resources . . . the result is that boys and girls have little or no music experience of either immediate or lasting value. [4]

Those who supported the music specialist position on this issue have been vocal down through the years (see pp. 69-70). In 1961 the *Saturday Review* described the elementary teacher's work as extraordinarily difficult: "She is expected to do too many things, play too many different roles, teach too many subjects, and to display an array of talents rarely found in a single individual." [5] Also in 1961, Burnsworth wrote: "Widespread practice and the majority of professional opinions continue to encourage and support the belief that the regular classroom teacher is adequate to the task, yet both history and research dispute this position." [6] Many research studies reveal that when classroom teachers are asked what they think about this issue, from 60 to 80 per cent reply that music is a special subject best taught by music specialists, thus implying strongly that they believe they should not be expected to teach it. In reply to those who claimed that "anybody can teach music," Oleta Benn wrote: "Some may argue that in order to teach young children one need not be much of a musician. If someone is able to 'carry a tune,' he is con-

---

[1] Alfred Ellison, *Music With Children* (New York: McGraw-Hill Book Company, Inc., 1959), p. 1.

[2] *Ibid.*, p. 249.

[3] James L. Mursell, *Music and the Classroom Teacher* (New York: Silver Burdett Company, 1951), p. 71.

[4] Marguerite V. Hood, "Our Changing School Music Program," *Music Educators Journal* (February-March, 1962), 50.

[5] The Editor's Bookshelf, *Saturday Review* (December 16, 1961), 54.

[6] Charles C. Burnsworth, "The Self-Contained Classroom Reconsidered," *Music Educators Journal* (November-December, 1961), 41.

sidered fit. It seems appalling to propose that ignorance of a subject be a recommendation for teaching it." [7]

Chester Squire's 1962 study includes principals' ratings of 28 teaching competencies. In this study, music was rated 28th, or the competency most lacking in elementary teachers.[8] Interestingly enough, 21 per cent of the classroom teacher respondents declared their college preparation was "more than adequate" for the kind of music teaching they did,[9] while only one-third of these respondents declared that they were insufficiently prepared for the music teaching they were expected to do.[10] According to Newton: "The greatest per cent (of classroom teachers) not able to teach their own music lies beyond the 50th percentile." [11] Jack Schaeffer, Supervisor of Music in the Seattle, Washington, schools writes:

> It is true that *some* of our best classroom teachers can teach music just as they are able to teach many other subjects in a skillful manner. We are just as convinced that there are *many more* classroom teachers who are not able to teach their own music. . . . The need for specialization in this area is more logical and more essential than in any other area of the curriculum.[12]

Burmeister lists the minimum competencies necessary for the teaching of elementary school music:

> (a) a positive attitude toward teaching music; (b) ability to use the singing voice accurately and with reasonably pleasant quality; (c) functional piano facility; (d) ability to teach a rote song; (e) knowledge of the elements of notation; (f) basic knowledge about voice and instruments; (g) a repertoire of good songs suitable for the level taught; (h) a knowledge of fine music literature to draw on for resource material.[13]

---

[7] Oleta A. Benn, as quoted by *The Washington Music Educator* (February, 1960), 59.

[8] Chester C. Squire, "An Evaluation of the Elementary Teacher Education Program at Southern Oregon College," (Doctoral dissertation presented at the University of Oregon, 1962), p. 134.

[9] *Ibid.*, p. 138.

[10] *Ibid.*, p. 167.

[11] Margaret Newton, "A Resumé of a Survey Miss Newton Conducted as Co-Chairman of the Minnesota Committee on Music for Elementary Teachers," *Gopher Music Notes* (April, 1953).

[12] Jack E. Schaeffer, "Need for Music Specialists," *Washington Music Educator* (Spring, 1961), 7.

[13] A. Burmeister, "The Role of Music in General Education," in *Basic Concepts in Music Education*, Nelson B. Henry, ed. (Chicago: The University of Chicago Press, 1958), p. 226.

He states that a teacher with these minimum competencies should, by working with a music specialist, be able to achieve a proper balance between music as a general cultural subject and music as a skill. He adds that no state requires an adequate minimum of preparation for this teaching. Hoffer and English are of the opinion that the relation of the classroom teacher and the music specialist is supplementary: "The specialist does those things which the teacher has not the training to do, and the teacher handles music activities which cannot be worked into the crowded schedule of the specialist." They list nine activities that the classroom teacher should reasonably be able to do, even though the specialist will be responsible for deciding "the form, materials, overall timing, and general methods"—thus implying a type of supervisory authority on the part of the specialist.[14]

Numerous studies reveal that classroom teachers state "lack of time" as a major barrier to successful music teaching. Hoffer and English trace this to the lack of preparation to teach the subject, which results in the fact that the average teacher must go through a laborious process of identifying the rhythm and pitches and gradually teaching herself the song. They believe that very few teachers are willing, in view of all the other demands made upon their time, to involve themselves to such an extent in preparing a lesson in music.[15]

Since musical competence is determined in large part by a person's musical education both in and out of school, attempts to correct musical deficiencies in later years have met with uneven success. In most subject areas, a teacher can grow professionally in the customary manner. In music, studying from books is only part of a professional growth which also includes performance. As one principal put it: "In most subjects a teacher might stand up with a book, but in music she must stand up with a book *and sing!*" People who feel inadequate in an activity are not happy with it and tend to avoid it. Psychology tells us that it is basically wrong to expect a teacher to teach from a position of inadequacy. The teacher who lacks musical competence is usually the one who does not enroll in college classes and summer workshops unless forced to do so by

---

14 Charles R. Hoffer and Catherine A. English, "The Music Specialist and the Classroom Teacher," *Music Educators Journal* (September-October, 1961), 46.
15 *Ibid.*, p. 48.

state certification requirements or by local school officials. Conversely, the teacher who is musical and who enjoys music and is happy and successful in it, voluntarily enrolls in summer classes and workshops. In short, although some interesting efforts have been put forth to assist growth in music-teaching competency, they have generally been insufficient to counteract a basic lack of musical compétency resulting either from lack of natural ability in music or from meager contact with musical education in the home and elementary-school environment.

As for the specialist, he is currently in great demand—a demand which has grown steadily in recent years. Teacher placement service figures show that of all types of music positions, that of the elementary specialist is in shortest supply in relation to a growing number of openings. Such a specialist not only needs to know music, but he must also understand child growth and development and its relation to music, have a general understanding of the elementary curriculum, and be able to recognize and accommodate the many individual differences found in children. His is indeed a complex task. Russel Squire writes: "If music teaching in the schools is to be genuinely significant, thoroughly trained musicians must be placed in charge." [16] William Hartshorn, Supervisor of Music in the Los Angeles schools, states: "The increasing use of music specialists at this level has not disturbed the good balance [of the curriculum]. In fact, it has served to upgrade the quality of instruction for *all* pupils." [17]

Teacher preparation in music requires little course work versus teacher education in music requires extensive course work. Remarks bearing upon this issue have appeared throughout this book. Cykler states that prospective teachers in Austria and Germany have had from twelve to thirteen years of school music instruction before they start their professional training. He contrasts the American colleges' requirement of one semester to one year of musical education with the five years of collegiate musical training in the Austrian Teacher Training Institutes. He states that the musical competency of these candidates for elementary teacher training is

---

[16] Russel N. Squire, *Introduction to Music Education* (New York: The Ronald Press, 1952), p. 16.
[17] William C. Hartshorn, "The Music Curriculum Present and Future," *Music Educators Journal* (April-May, 1961), 42.

likely to be far in advance of that of the American students, owing to their many years of continuous musical training.[18]

The very extensive musical education of the Austro-German classroom teacher is of interest when contrasted with the comparatively meager training of his American counterpart because these teachers are expected to have about the same competencies. However, this point need not be labored further, since research is in agreement that the average classroom teacher of music in the United States needs far more education in music than he now has in order to be able to teach it satisfactorily. Research further points out the areas of creativity, part-singing, notation, provision for individual differences, and remedial work as being notably absent in the on-the-job performance of the American teacher. It describes music when taught by this teacher as being largely rote singing and a little listening. This reflects not only the serious lack of continuity and organization of some music programs from kindergarten through the college years, but also the content of the brief collegiate training required. This writer does not know to what extent the college music class should be held responsible for this apparent failure in American education. To be a music teacher requires lengthy and continuous training. The American educational system has not generally operated in this fashion, yet in many schools the classroom teacher is expected to be able to teach music—a subject for which he lacks experience and training. A college course of a semester or a year, no matter how well taught, can not be expected to compensate for poor musical experiences, or for a lack of continuity of musical experiences. However, colleges can be held accountable for such practices as requiring the elementary education major to take courses in music which lack content relating to the teaching the student will be doing in the public school classroom and assigning the teaching of these courses to instructors who have never taught elementary school music.

Research reveals that one of the most obvious points of weakness in the existing college preparatory courses is in the area of student teaching. Surveys show that one-third or more of the student teachers have very little or no experience in the student teaching of music.

---

[18] Edmund Cykler, "Some Salient Areas of Comparison in the Training of Music Teachers in Austria, Germany, and the United States of America," *International Music Educator* (November, 1960), 32-33.

The reasons are: (1) a music specialist teaches the music and makes no effort to aid the student teacher; (2) the teacher in whose self-contained classroom the student teacher is placed is not musically competent and omits music from her program of studies; (3) the general college supervisor is not competent in music and is happy to avoid any reference to it when supervising the student. The result is that a pattern of *not* teaching music sometimes becomes established before the student has graduated from college.

Because of the lack of continuity in American music education, some college courses in music must of necessity be remedial and often cannot be considered to be of college level although college credits are usually granted. In areas where the elementary and secondary schools fail to provide a good music program, the college should seek some means of examining the native musical ability of each applicant who desires to enter the elementary teacher education program. Then remedial classes in voice and in keyboard experience should be provided for those students in need of them. The music methods course is subject to the same criticism which is made of most other college methods courses: there is usually insufficient immediate relation of the course content to the teaching of children. To make methods courses more practical learning experiences, the student should have opportunity to observe and participate in teaching children each aspect of the elementary music program as it is presented in the college class.

The education of the music specialist has been mentioned earlier. Because of the nature of the learning process in music, and because of the several types of positions the music graduate is called upon to fill, the concentration of work in the major area is heavier than in most other subject fields. Of prime importance is the musical training and the professional training and orientation. These two aspects consume so many credit hours of college work that a music major cannot be expected to have as much general education as is usually required in teacher training curricula for "academic" subjects. This is, however, still a matter of controversy.

When the opinions concerning the value of music courses to classroom teachers and music specialists are compared, it is of interest that the classroom teacher places methods first in importance, followed by knowledge of basic music (fundamentals) and music literature (appreciation), while the music major places basic music (theory) first in importance, with music literature second, and methods of teaching third. Apparently, those who know the basic subject matter of music best rate it as first in importance, while those who lack this knowledge regard it as secondary to teaching methods.

Another interesting research finding is evidence that the more one knows about a subject, the more need he discovers for additional education and assistance in it. This may be true in all areas of knowledge. For example, in one experimental study undertaken in a college, the instructor spent two and one-half times as many hours with an experimental group as she did with students in the regular teacher education program. The result was that most of the students in the regular program were of the opinion that too much time and too many credits were allotted to the course, while most of the students in the experimental group complained that the instructor was unable to give them as much time and help as they needed.

As part of a Master of Science program at the University of Utah in 1945, Morgan K. Lund made an interesting observation concerning two groups of sixteen classroom teachers, one group well-prepared musically, and the other group ill-prepared. In his thesis, *A Study of Music Preparation of Elementary Teachers in the Granite School District,* he states:

> One peculiar result is that nine of the high group feel they need more training in music, while only two of the low group feel such need. It would seem that the order should be reversed. Evidently, those knowing more about music can see more need for certain types of training, while those who lack such knowledge concerning music are unaware of their needs.

That elementary music specialists need additional training or orientation is implied by the Anderson study, which concludes that the specialists in certain selected schools in Illinois had not succeeded in realizing objectives recommended by experts in music education. For example, the provision of opportunities for creative experience was believed to have been neglected in their teaching.[19]

Plans of organization based primarily upon the specialist versus plans of organization based primarily upon the classroom teacher. Between 1838 and 1885, music teaching was primarily

---

[19] Virginia N. Anderson, "The Status of Music in Elementary Schools in Illinois" (unpublished master's thesis presented at Illinois Wesleyan University, 1955), p. 102.

the domain of the specialist. Between 1885 and 1910, the emphasis turned toward the classroom teacher. After 1910 the pendulum swung slowly back toward the specialist until the self-contained classroom concept turned it back again. In view of this fairly regular fluctuation, it would seem possible or even probable that a turn toward the specialist is now due.

The common plans of organization are:

1. The classroom teacher, unassisted, teaches music.
2. The classroom teacher, assisted by a music specialist not on schedule, teaches music.
3. The classroom teacher, under supervision of a specialist, teaches music.
4. The classroom teacher teaches music in the primary grades with some specialist help, and the specialist teaches music in the intermediate grades (usually beginning with Grade 4).
5. The music specialist teaches the entire music program with some assistance from classroom teachers who teach music the days he is not present.
6. The music specialist teaches the entire music program with no assistance.

Attempts to resolve this issue have been made difficult by a near-absence of attempts at the local school level to determine progress or lack of progress in achieving the objectives of music programs, and by the rigid opinions of those who approach the problem as though there is only one possible plan of organization, or as though their present plan of organization will always remain unchanged in the midst of an ever-changing educational system. Some of these people can see no faults—only virtues—in the music specialist plan. Others accept the self-contained classroom on faith rather than as an organizational plan which, like any other plan, is subject to constant study, evaluation, and subsequent reorganization. The author recalls being instructed; "Under no circumstances can we [music educators] admit that any classroom teacher cannot teach music." Today we should know that problems must be faced openly and directly if they are to be solved.

A study which deals with school administrators' opinions on this issue was made in the school year 1958–59 in Texas. It was found that 41 per cent of Texas schools used specialists for the music instruction in all the elementary grades; 26 per cent used specialists in the intermediate grades only; 20 per cent used only classroom teachers, with or without assistance; and 13 per cent used specialists beginning at the fifth grade level. A large majority of 87 per cent of the school superintendents favored the teaching of music by specialists. More than thirty of the respondents added remarks to the effect that music *must* be taught by specialists if children are to receive adequate instruction in the subject. Thirty respondents commented that specialists were not teaching the music in their schools because of financial reasons. Twenty-four per cent of the superintendents stated that their school districts had definite plans to employ additional specialists, while 2 per cent stated that their districts planned to terminate the use of specialists. Twelve reported difficulties in obtaining specialists to fill positions. Slightly more than half the Texas administrators believed that there was a trend toward employment of specialists to teach music, and one-fourth of Texas school districts were reported to have definite plans either to increase or to initiate the use of music specialists.[20]

Available research shows that both school administrators and music specialists favor the teaching of music by specialists.

This writer failed to find research which would indicate clearly that the classroom teacher needs more or less basic musical competence in music teaching at any particular grade level, although common practice often assigns music instruction to the room teacher in Grades 1, 2, and 3, while the specialist has this assignment in Grades 4, 5, and 6. Part-singing and added complexity of song material and listening activities are assumed to be reasons for the division of responsibility at this point. However, teaching music properly in the primary grades demands substantial musical abilities and knowledges. This is frequently overlooked by general educators and music educators alike.

An interesting study was conducted in a local school district in a city of 50,000 people. About 300 classroom teachers were assisted by two consultants who had no supervisory authority; the principals were the supervisory officers in all areas of instruction. The major conclusion was that the results of this organizational plan were substandard. The teachers and principals gave the following opinions for this situation, in order of frequency:

[20] Lawrence H. McQuerrey, "Elementary Special Music Teachers in Texas," *Music Educators Journal* (November-December, 1959), 60.

1. Lack of time in which to plan and carry out an adequate music program.

2. Lack of musical competence on the part of the average classroom teacher.

3. Relative dislike of music teaching by a large minority of classroom teachers.

4. Inability of classroom teachers to teach effectively many or most aspects of a balanced music program.

5. Failure of the teachers to reduce the proportion of children unable to sing accurately on pitch as they progressed from grade to grade (Grade 1: 18 per cent, Grade 6: 17 per cent).

The principals stated the three major strengths of this organizational plan to be, in order of frequency of response:

1. Supports the concept of the self-contained classroom.

2. Permits maximum correlation of music with other areas.

3. Provides the services of the music consultant, which are excellent.

(Note that none of the above reasons are concerned with achievement in music skills, understandings, or appreciations.)

They gave as the two major weaknesses of this plan:

1. The inability of classroom teachers to teach music properly.
2. Classroom teacher disinterest in teaching music.

Team teaching has been recently introduced in some schools. This is often a somewhat different approach to specialization, and permits a teacher who is competent in music to reach more children. In music it appears to operate somewhat like the older "trading of subjects" plan in which a teacher who could not teach music asked a fellow teacher to take her class in music while she taught the other teacher's class in a subject in which she felt competent.

The supervisor versus the consultant. This issue is not easily stated because of the confusion of titles and responsibilities involved in these school positions. The true issue revolves around the degree of authority possessed and exercised, regardless of the specific title. In their extreme interpretations, the supervisor is one who controls, directs, and exercises authority, while the consultant is one who assists largely on an on-call basis, and who possesses no authority to direct anyone. "Leadership" is asserted to be an important function of persons who occupy either of these positions.

Historically, authoritarian supervision was deemed necessary in any area in which teachers lacked competence. In early American education, most classroom teachers were assumed to lack general competence, and principals exercised the rigid controls necessary in this situation. When the special subjects of music, art, and physical education came into being, the principal was found to be not sufficiently educated in them to be capable of supervising them, so specialists were appointed as supervisors. As the education of classroom teachers improved, supervision relaxed its authoritarian nature. Of course, throughout the history of supervision there have always been kindly and helpful supervisors who knew that their function was to improve the education of children by encouraging the professional growth of teachers. However, the better educated teacher who did not seem to require direct supervision, the concept of a unified learning environment without artificially segmented parts, and the self-contained classroom plan of organization combined to cast doubts upon supervision generally. As one principal stated:

> The supervisory system includes the spectre of being rated by a superior. This may result in personality conflicts and personal clashes, which means in turn a less than professional appraisal by the supervisor. In my school, a very good personal relationship now exists between the *consultants* and the teachers.

In the reaction against the directive form of supervision, the supervisor of music in many school districts was relieved of any direct authority over music, and this authority was placed in the hands of the principal. In some situations, persuasion and friendliness became the only means through which the ex-supervisor, now consultant, could operate. Research shows that the average classroom teacher today is not sufficiently competent to teach music. Since lack of competence was the historical basis for establishing supervision, it is interesting to note that American music education today in some schools is operating upon a different basic assumption. This seems to be that if a consultant is friendly and lacks authority, the classroom teacher will react in a strongly professional manner to improve her teaching. Thus, the assumed lack of tension will automatically cause the two to work together to improve the education of children. The school district study already discussed (see p. 95) revealed that personal relations between staff members were very good. In view of the labelling of the music program in that district as substandard, the doubter may say: "Even though staff relations are very important in their effect upon the quality of children's education, still more important is the achievement of children in their education. Since research reveals that music as taught by the average classroom teacher is substandard or even nonexistent, what good to the children comes from these 'good staff relations' as far as their education in music is concerned?" This is a question which must eventually be answered in school systems of this type.

Andrews and Cockerille insist that supervision is not necessarily rigid in its application, stating:

> The music specialists and administrators who are aware of the human relations aspects of this organization of work can achieve rapport with the classroom teachers, with the result that the visit of the Music Supervisor becomes a pleasant, challenging educational experience.[21]

By focusing attention on the child, the professionally-oriented supervisor and teacher should be able to work together in a healthy relationship from which children can benefit.

That teachers generally do not desire supervision is one facet of a 1949 study, which shows strong classroom teacher support for the consultant-type supervisory arrangement. These teachers claimed the advantages of the consultant plan to be: (1) a more cooperative and democratic relationship between the teacher and consultant, (2) a more extensive correlation of music and other areas, and (3) a larger degree of professional growth among teachers. The disadvantages were stated as (1) lack of pupil skill in note reading and playing classroom instruments, (2) lack of music training or ability of classroom teachers, and (3) lack of time for overworked consultants to help teachers who need assistance. The study found that little attempt was being made to evaluate the results of music consultant plans of supervision.[22]

In the 1960 report on the music program in New York City

---

[21] Frances M. Andrews and Clara E. Cockerille, *Your School Music Program: A Guide to Effective Curriculum Development* (Englewood Cliffs, N.J.: Prentice-Hall, Inc., 1958), p. 78.

[22] Robert E. Nye, "Critical Survey and Evaluation of Practices in Cooperative Supervision of Music in the Elementary School" (Doctoral dissertation presented at the University of Wisconsin, 1949), p. 78.

Schools, "insufficient supervision" was cited as one of the factors which limit the effectiveness of the elementary music program:

> The immediate supervision of classroom activities is the responsibility of the principal. . . . The fact must be faced, however, that since 1939, when special teachers of music were relieved of their supervisory duties and assigned to regular teaching positions, the program has suffered greatly.[23]

The words of Superintendent John Theobald in the Foreward of the Report further explains the problem:

> It is my hope that the program may be strengthened on all levels, particularly the elementary level where the teaching of music is entrusted to regular classroom teachers, many of whom have insufficient training, knowledge or ability in this highly specialized subject.

The Hertz study concluded that the average principal does not supervise his teachers well enough to determine accurately their strengths and weaknesses—that time to allow such supervision evidently does not exist. Hertz advised that the deficiencies in the area of music were such that special consideration must be given to that area of teacher preparation.[24]

In 1952 Fowler Smith said that if a grade teacher is to teach music, then more supervision is necessary. He added that good teachers welcome supervision, that poor teachers cannot get along without it, and that supervision is "grand work" if it is "democratic, inspirational leadership that opens up new and expanding horizons." He declared that we owe the present status of music in the schools to the supervisors "who have fought, bled, and died for the cause." [25] In 1958 Karl Ernst said: "The music program in any school will not achieve beyond the insight and vision of the administrator." [26] Leonhard and House claim that "Supervision of music is essentially a task for the music specialist." [27] An anonymous administrator writes: "The trouble is that we do not have administrators and super-

---

[23] "Music: A Report on the Program in New York City Schools," Board of Education, New York City, June 30, 1960, p. 14.

[24] Wayne S. Hertz, "The Relationship Between the Teaching Success of First-Year Elementary Teachers and Their Undergraduate Preparation" (Doctoral dissertation presented at New York University, July, 1959).

[25] Fowler Smith, "Supervision," *Music Educators Journal* (June-July, 1952), 34.

[26] Karl Ernst, "The Music Teacher Looks at the Principal," *National Education Association Journal* (May, 1958), 330-31.

[27] Charles Leonhard and Robert W. House, *Foundations and Principles of Music Education* (New York: McGraw-Hill Book Company, Inc., 1959), p. 307.

visors big enough to lead (draw out) and at the same time *direct* teachers. We (I include myself) are not big enough for the role which American education has set for itself." [28]

In recent years there have been a number of evaluations of American schools by lay committees and by professors in the academic disciplines. Mackenzie writes, "In some instances, the supervisory staffs in school systems were not even consulted as changes of various kinds were introduced by boards of education. It is probably safe to say that thousands of supervisors felt by-passed." [29] The changes he mentions resulted from the evaluations made by the lay committees and the professors, neither of these being public school-oriented in the professional sense. He adds that the role of the supervisor needs clarification. Tiffany states that the services of a supervisor are sought by the secure teacher, and that any supervisor should "bring more to the teacher than he expects from the teacher" in order to win acceptance by teachers. He notes with some concern a trend toward the taking over of former supervisory functions by helping teachers, special teachers, and master teachers, and questions whether this type of personnel has adequate preparation to supervise. He also wants the jobs of principal and supervisor defined, and claims that many of those who now bear the title of "supervisor," "consultant," or "coordinator" find themselves in a professional "no man's land." [30] Mursell writes that if the specialist should not function as a supervisor, his status must still be defined. "His relationship to the work cannot be merely permissive, or his whole status becomes impossible and his potential contribution is sabotaged from the start." [31]

When businessmen serve on lay committees to study school problems, their reaction may often be summarized as: "Supervision is essential in my business. My employees expect to be supervised. This seems to be lacking in the schools." Although there are many

---

[28] Robert E. Nye, "Critical Survey and Evaluation of Practices in Cooperative Supervision of Music in the Elementary School" (Doctoral dissertation presented at the University of Wisconsin, 1949), p. 126.

[29] Gordon N. Mackenzie, "Recent Developments in the Role of the Supervisor," *Educational Leadership* (November, 1961), 88-89.

[30] Burton C. Tiffany, "Improving Skills in Working with School Personnel," *Educational Leadership* (November, 1961), 92-93.

[31] James L. Mursell, *Music Education Principles and Programs* (New York: Silver Burdett Company, 1956), p. 354.

things about business and education which cannot be rightly compared, there is food for thought in such comments.

The music program planned in terms of classroom teacher competence versus the music program planned in terms of children's capabilities.

> The elementary school music program has plagued music educators and school officials, in some views, more than any other phase of public school music. While headway has been made in other aspects of the program, the elementary music problems are in many respects the same as they were fifty or more years ago.[32]

The writer of those words added that it is unfortunate for music that the musical learnings in the elementary school are the most important aspect of the twelve-year program.

The trend toward the teaching of music by the classroom teacher carried with it the assumption that this teacher would be prepared to teach music. Educational historians pointed to the fact that arithmetic was once a special subject taught by specialists, but now every elementary teacher is assumed to be competent in this subject. Some of these historians have predicted that music would become one of the areas in which the room teacher has full competence. However, this has not occurred—the average room teacher has not achieved this competence. In this situation, the question of redefining the content of the music program was certain to arise. Most classroom teachers look upon a program designed in accordance with children's musical capacities as impractical because they cannot, with their limited musical training, bring its objectives to fruition. The frustration which results is well-known to administrators, most of whom prefer not to deal with it in a supervisory capacity. Unless teacher competence is somehow improved, the logical result will be a lowering of the objectives of the music program in keeping with the level of abilities of the average classroom teacher. Yet, it is obviously indefensible to plan any worthy educational program on anything but children's natural capacities and needs.

That the average classroom teacher is not capable of teaching a balanced music program has already been asserted. Among the many aspects of music which classroom teachers commonly point

---

[32] Charles C. Burnsworth, "The Self-Contained Classroom Reconsidered," *Music Educators Journal* (November-December, 1961), 41.

out as being most difficult are the study of notation and part-singing. Some schools solved this problem by simply reducing their objectives to eliminate these aspects. A few college textbooks obliged by deëmphasizing one or both of them, on the grounds that most classroom teachers would be unable to teach them. Since musically-educated persons cannot comprehend how music can be taught without many references to, and frequent uses of, notation, this issue was quickly joined. The same was true with part-singing, which to the musically-educated is a normal part of children's development which cannot be denied in any worthy music program. Music has been described as a picture of sound painted on a canvas of silence. Since notation is simply an ingenious illustration of what one hears, it aids comprehension—and therefore learning—in the same way illustrations assist comprehension in other areas of instruction. Thus, it would seem strange indeed that anyone would propose to eliminate it from any music program.

There is a question as to the extent to which genuine *programs* of music education exist in many elementary schools today. A recently retired professor of education, Dr. Nicholas Moseley, and his wife began a leisurely drive from New England to Florida in the fall of 1958. Enroute they visited many schools to collect materials for a textbook he was writing. After arriving in Florida he wrote: "We are appalled at how little music there is—at the extent to which the classroom teacher leaves everything to a music supervisor, and if there is no specialist, the extent to which music is ignored altogether."

A common question concerning the music program is: To what extent should it be interrelated with other subject areas? Most classroom teachers understand this use of music well, but they often confuse it with a music education program. Also, interrelating can sometimes be an excuse for never teaching music as musicians recognize the subject. Confusion surrounding this issue is illustrated by the fact that at least one state and at least one large city system publish courses of study which rule that music may be taught *only* as a part of an integrated curriculum, correlated with other subjects.[34] Preston, writing in the social studies field, states that integration should never be forced: "A class which is studying Switzerland,

---

[34] John J. Prihoda, "A Survey of Elementary School Music Courses of Study" (Master's thesis presented at Northern Illinois University, 1959), pp. 16-18.

Riverside City College Library
Riverside, California

for example, is under no obligation, during music periods, to learn Swiss folk songs—unless other circumstances justify doing this." [35] Among the circumstances he mentions are that Swiss songs may be useful in achieving certain musical objectives of the music lesson, and that in the social studies lesson, the content of certain Swiss songs may help explain Swiss national life. He maintains that while social studies can serve well as an organizing center, it should do so "without blurring the identity of music or any other subject, each of which must still be systematically planned and taught by itself." Hartshorn reminds us that "Music will serve other subject fields best when its own integrity as an art is maintained." [36]

It seems apparent that while what constitutes a good music program for boys and girls has been clearly defined, lack of teacher competency in music often prevents its realization.

Summary

Will Durant, the philosopher, has defined civilization as a social order which promotes cultural creation. It consists of four elements: economic provision, political organization, moral traditions, and the pursuit of knowledge and the arts. He further states that language and knowledge, morals and manners, technology and the arts must all be provided through education in order to sustain civilization.[37]

According to educational history in the United States, the major responsibility for teaching music has passed twice back and forth from music specialist to classroom teacher. Today there are evidences that this imaginary pendulum may be continuing its periodic swing, this time again toward more specialization in the teaching of music. The condition of the classroom teacher with regard to numerous duties, insufficient time, and inadequate preparation to teach music seems to remain almost constant over the years of this century. The type of school that departmentalizes music is still a thriving institution. It has escaped many of the problems with which this monograph has been concerned, and those who are in adminis-

---

[35] Ralph C. Preston, *Teaching Social Studies in the Elementary School,* rev. ed. (New York: Holt, Rinehart & Winston, Inc., 1958), p. 8.

[36] William C. Hartshorn, "The Role of Listening," in *Basic Concepts in Music Education,* Nelson B. Henry, ed. (Chicago: University of Chicago Press, 1958), p. 285.

[37] Will Durant, *Our Oriental Heritage* (New York: Simon and Schuster, 1935), pp. 1-4.

trative authority in these schools generally have no desire to change to a wholly self-contained classroom situation. At one time the administrator was the over-all supervisor. Later, specialists were appointed to supervise the specialized areas—including music—because the principal lacked the competence to properly supervise these areas. Today, in many schools, the supervisory authority over special areas is again assigned to the principal, whether or not he may be sufficiently prepared to carry out this assignment.

Burnsworth writes an interesting summary in which he claims that the development of the self-contained classroom created the need for adequate preparation in music for the classroom teacher. He further claims that in an attempt to "idealize" the plan, much was written to support the theory that the classroom teacher needed little music training to teach music well. He believes that this effort to condition the classroom teacher psychologically contributed to a strong suspicion that even the professional music educator did not need very much intelligence or education to be a music teacher—"a belief that many music educators are now finding themselves forced to refute." He states that this line of thought affected the attitude of college personnel responsible for curriculum planning, some of whom now feel that one or two basic courses in music should be sufficient for the teacher candidate. He interprets what took place as an innocent justification for allowing classroom teachers to conduct their own music programs rather than have music dropped from the curriculum, and believes that from this has developed a mistaken concept that could undermine good music education programs on both public school and collegiate levels.[38]

Allen Britton warns the music educator about agreeing too readily with whatever general education may next decide to do. He writes:

> And to the present day many American music educators have demonstrated what may be considered an easy readiness to climb aboard any intellectual bandwagon which happened to be near by, and trust it to arrive at destinations appropriate for music educators, or worse, to adopt its destinations as their own without careful enough scrutiny of the intellectual proprieties involved.[39]

[38] Charles C. Burnsworth, "The Self-Contained Classroom Reconsidered," *Music Educators Journal* (November-December, 1961), 41.

[39] Allen P. Britton, "Music in Early American Public Education: A Historical Critique," in *Basic Concepts in Music Education, op. cit.,* p. 207.

He warns us to be more critical of new practices and to be more certain that they are applicable to music education.

When seeking solutions for our problems, we must not permit popular caricatures to blind us to facts. These include such stereotypes as the specialist who is entirely ignorant of child development, the laws of learning, and human relations; the supervisor who does nothing but terrify teachers; the classroom teacher who is invariably musically competent (or incompetent); the principal who knows everything about everything (or nothing about anything). These are so far from presenting a true picture that they are only ridiculous. All younger teachers today have much the same basic professional education no matter what their fields of work may be. The music specialist probably has more professional preparation than most subject matter specialists because he often takes methods courses on both elementary and secondary levels.

There is a belief that students often forgive a poor teacher of an academic subject but find it less possible to forgive a poor teacher of music, possibly because music is an area filled with feelings and emotions. The specialist as well as the classroom teacher should be able to tell when facts and techniques of music should be taught, for if the child is given technical training before he has need of it, he cannot assimilate it and may lose interest in the subject. However, if the child is ready for technical training and this need remains unsatisfied, his interest and creativity vanish because he cannot function musically at his true level. It requires *many* skills and knowledges to be a good music teacher.

Research has shown that the large majority of classroom teachers, administrators, and music educators support the concept of music as a special subject to be taught by specialists. Then, why has this concept not been accepted universally? The reason most commonly stated is a financial one—that there is not sufficient money to pay for specialists in some school systems. Since music is officially recognized by the U.S. Office of Education and by the state departments of education as a part of the general education program for the youth of the nation, why should there not be money to implement this program? Music would seem to deserve its share of the available funds in accordance with how the program must be organized and administered to be effective. Since situations have been observed in which insufficient funds did not permit the employment of special music teachers, but in which funds were later found to employ numerous additions of other types to the school staff, it can be suspected that finances do not tell the whole story. A more logical theory is that the methods of teaching music in some schools have not made its values sufficiently apparent to build strongly enough the concept of music as an essential subject. One hears classroom teachers remark: "The more important subjects must be taught first, and then, if there is time. . . ." Another theory places the responsibility for this situation at the door of boards of education.

In some schools, poor methods of teaching music have caused the program to go the way of a descending spiral. When quality dwindles far enough, there is little of value worth retaining, and the program is then ripe for abandonment. After all, education exists to help children learn those things which cannot be normally learned directly from their out-of-school environment.

The hope for the future of public school music may lie with the large minority of schools that departmentalize elementary music. The specialists who teach in these schools, if they are properly prepared for their exacting and important work, are in a strategic position from which to begin a major advance in music education. If they, through excellent teaching, succeed in making the values of music to children clearly apparent, then they will lead the way toward significant improvement in the level of elementary school music.

Knowledge of music is gained only through long and continuous musical education. If American education decides that the classroom teacher is to be the dominant figure in elementary school music after all, then changes will be made in the educational pattern of this teacher. In the first place, the childhood years in elementary and secondary schools will include a rich, satisfying, and consistently-organized music program. The collegiate years will have music as a continuous thread, and any student who lacks native musical ability will be barred from preparing to teach in elementary schools. The school of the future will not employ a teacher who cannot teach music acceptably, and if one who is not musical is somehow employed through error, he will not be allowed to remain in that position. Theoretically, the classroom teacher may be the best person to teach music. Practically, this theory has failed because of inadequate musical training, and employment practices in the schools which admitted musically incapable teachers to positions which involved music teaching. If American education desires the classroom teacher to be competent and comfortable in the role of music teacher, it must take the steps necessary to bring this about. As Oleta Benn writes: "Thus do we prepare children for the day when they will decide what music means to them. They cannot make a valid judgment unless they have been recipients of truly musical development at the hands of a truly musical person." [40]

Finally, to quote Karl Gehrkens once more: "If music education is to succeed, the teacher must be a good musician, well-prepared to teach music, he must know, understand, and enjoy children, and there should be a large quantity of high-grade materials of instruction at his disposal." [41]

The future may have in store for American schools a music program in which the teaching is shared by specialists and classroom teachers, each musically competent to do those things which he is best prepared to do. Both specialists and classroom teachers have important responsibilities in music. Education should make plans to bring this into reality for the sake of the children's maximum aesthetic development.

---

[40] Oleta Benn, "Esthetics for the Music Educator: The Maturation of the Esthetic Sense," *Journal of Research in Music Education* (Fall, 1956), 131.

[41] Karl W. Gehrkens, "Five Decades of Music Education," *Education*, (March, 1956), 407.

Bibliography

Andrews, Frances M., and Clara E. Cockerille, *Your School Music Program.* Englewood Cliffs, N.J.: Prentice-Hall, Inc., 1958.

Birge, Edward B., *History of Public School Music in the United States.* Philadelphia: Oliver Ditson Company, 1939.

Britton, Allen P., ed., *Music Education Materials: A Selected Bibliography.* Washington, D.C.: Music Educators National Conference, 1959.

Careers in Music (brochure). Washington, D.C.: Music Educators National Conference, 1956.

Cutts, Norma E., and Nicholas Mosely, *Providing for Individual Differences in the Elementary School.* Chapter 6, "Music," Englewood Cliffs, N.J.: Prentice-Hall, Inc., 1960.

Henry, Nelson B. ed., *Basic Concepts in Music Education:* The Fifty-Seventh Yearbook of the National Society for the Study of Education. Chicago: University of Chicago Press, 1958. Vol. 1.

Leonhard, Charles, and Robert W. House, *Foundations and Principles of Music Education.* New York: McGraw-Hill Book Company, Inc., 1959.

Mathews, Paul Wentworth, *You Can Teach Music.* New York: E. P. Dutton and Co., Inc., 1953.

Mursell, James L., *Music and the Classroom Teacher.* New York: Silver Burdett Company, 1951.

————, *Music Education Principles and Programs.* New York: Silver Burdett Company, 1956.

Music Education for Elementary School Children. Washington, D.C.: Music Educators National Conference, 1960.

Music Education in Oregon Public Schools. Salem, Oregon: The State Department of Education, 1960.

Nye, Robert E., and Bjornar Bergethon, *Basic Music for Classroom Teachers,* 2nd ed. Englewood Cliffs, N.J.: Prentice-Hall, Inc., 1962.

Nye, Robert E., and Vernice Trousdale Nye, *Music in the Elementary School.* Englewood Cliffs, N.J.: Prentice-Hall, Inc., 1957, 1964.

Nye, Robert E., Vernice Nye, Neva Aubin, and George Kyme, *Singing With Children.* Belmont, California: Wadsworth Publishing Company, 1962.

Orff, Carl, and Gunild Keetman, *Music for Children.* Vols. 1, 2, 3. New York: Associated Music Publishers, Inc., 1956-62.

Pierce, Anne E., *Teaching Music in the Elementary School.* New York: Holt, Rinehart & Winston, Inc., 1959.

Sheehy, Emma D., *Children Discover Music and Dance.* New York: Holt, Rinehart & Winston, Inc., 1959.

Shetler, Donald J., *Film Guide for Music Educators*. Washington, D.C.: Music Educators National Conference, 1961.

Snyder, Keith D., *School Music Administration and Supervision*. Boston: Allyn and Bacon, Inc., 1959.

Swanson, Bessie R., *Music in the Education of Children*. Belmont, California: Wadsworth Publishing Company. Inc., 1961.

Tooze, Ruth, and Beatrice Perham Krone, *Literature and Music as Resources for Social Studies*. Englewood Cliffs, N.J.: Prentice-Hall, Inc., 1955.

Index

Index